CARCASS
Furniture

LEABHARLA... ...H...
V...

Contents

INTRODUCTION   1

TIGHT CORNER   2
Brendan Devitt-Spooner makes a corner cabinet in English cherry

HEART OF OAK   8
Mark Constanduros creates a glazed-oak sideboard

QUICK ON THE DRAWER   13
Mike Cowie describes a limed chest of drawers he made at breakneck speed

GROOVY DRESSER
Mike Cowie makes a kitchen dresser with angled legs and burr
Part 1   17
Part 2   22

A JOINT VENTURE   26
Roswitha Lentge and Jeff Smith make an oak display cabinet

THROUGH A SIDE CABINET, DARKLY   32
Harold Wilson makes a mahogany side cabinet

COMPACT STORAGE   38
Derek Smith tidies away his music collection with this neat CD rack

CHEST BEATER   42
Mark Ripley makes a chest of drawers for a master bedroom

IN THEIR FOOTSTEPS   47
John Bullar makes an Arts and Crafts style cabinet

SPOONERISM   53
Brendan Devitt-Spooner makes a display cabinet, based on an earlier concept

TRADITION RECAPTURED   59
Mark Applegate creates a five-drawer oak and sycamore chest

BREAKFRONT WITH TRADITION   65
Brendan Devitt-Spooner designs an impressive breakfront cabinet

LABOUR FOR LOVE   71
Phillip Gullam makes a traditional dresser as a wedding gift

GOING GOTHIC   77
David Kortright makes a hi-fi cabinet in English oak

PERIOD DRAMA
Mike Cowie makes a classically inspired TV cabinet
Part 1   82
Part 2   87

AN INSPIRED PIECE   91
Andrew Lawton creates a clothes chest with an Arts and Crafts influence

KEEPER OF SECRETS   96
Duncan Lyall makes an English oak and sycamore chest of drawers with subtle curves

THE MACKINTOSH RECIPE
Neil McAllister recaptures the original style of his Edwardian house, while allowing for the needs of modern living
Part 1   102
Part 2   108
Part 3   114

METRIC/IMPERIAL CONVERSION CHART   119

INDEX   120

Note

Though every effort has been made to ensure that the information in this book is accurate at the time of writing, it is inevitable that prices, specifications and availability of some of the products mentioned will change from time to time. Readers are therefore urged to contact manufacturers or suppliers for up-to-date information before ordering.

Measurements

Although care has been taken to ensure that the metric measurements are true and accurate, they are only conversions from imperial; they have been rounded up or down to the nearest whole millimetre, or to the nearest convenient equivalent in cases where the imperial measurements themselves are only approximate. When following the projects, use either the metric or the imperial measurements; do not mix units.

Detailed conversion tables are provided on page 119.

Warning

All machine work is inherently dangerous unless suitable precautions are taken. Avoid loose clothing or hair which may catch in machinery. Protect your eyes and lungs against dust and flying debris by wearing goggles, dust mask or respirator as necessary, but invest in an efficient dust extractor as well.

Pay attention to electrical safety; in particular, do not use wet sanding or other techniques involving water unless your lathe is designed so that water cannot come into contact with the electrics.

Keep tools sharp; blunt tools are dangerous because they require more pressure and may behave unpredictably.

Do not work when your concentration is impaired by drugs, alcohol or fatigue.

The safety advice in this book is intended for your guidance, but cannot cover every eventuality: the safe use of machinery and tools is the responsibility of the user. If you are unhappy with a particular technique or procedure, do not use it – there is always another way.

Introduction

We all need storage space for the essentials in life, never mind all the stuff we would like to hide away. For most of us, space is a premium commodity. Simply because storage is such a basic need there is no reason why it should be mundane – the projects in this book prove that. The magazine that created the original articles and the projects chosen here represent a broad range. There is something here for everyone's home, whatever their taste in style. From large traditional dressers, to modern chests of drawers that will fit into different-sized homes, we have chosen pieces that will cover most aspects of storage in the house, including a kitchen.

Many of the makers whose pieces are here are professionals, but by no means all. Equally, the pieces use a variety of construction techniques that should mean most woodworkers would find something to suit their range of experience. There are also projects for those who feel they are bold enough to tackle more of a challenge!

The different makers all bring their own insight into furniture making and the pieces reflect that – something of the person who made it. Plenty to get your chisels into! From housings, to dovetails and glazing bars, the joints and methods are as varied as the individuals who made them. They encompass everything from solid sides to frame and panels, traditional to more modern techniques.

Happy making, and have fun!

Colin Eden-Eadon

Colin Eden-Eadon
Editor, *Furniture and Cabinetmaking*

PHOTOGRAPHY BY CHRIS SKARBON
ILLUSTRATIONS BY IAN HALL
AND SIMON RODWAY

Brendan Devitt-Spooner is a former teacher who turned to furniture-making and design in 1987. Largely self-taught, he takes a delight in using solid wood and has a preference for English timber

Tight corner

A corner cabinet in English cherry

Variation on a theme, a different angle on the corner cabinet

This style of cabinet first saw the light of day back in 1993. A long-term customer visited my workshop with a sketch proposal for a corner display cabinet.

The basic brief was for a corner cabinet with a single-glazed faceted door. At the drawing board it became apparent that the door was going to be the 'interesting' part of the project. As a general rule I do not make full-size drawings but make do with a scale drawing and appropriate sketches. But this time they were certainly needed – firstly to work out the size of the door components and, secondly, to use later on as a pattern on which to sit the door to check that all was well.

'If you make the door first and find that it is dimensionally slightly different to the drawing it is relatively easy to alter the carcass sides to accommodate this'

This cabinet was made for a Celebration of Craftsmanship Exhibition held at Cheltenham. The timber chosen was English cherry, with detail in laburnum. Although there are many other timbers that could have been used for the inlays, there are few English timbers that are naturally dark enough to give a good contrast.

Right way round

Although it is not the usual approach to making a cabinet with doors, I make the door first. When I did the first few of these cabinets I made the carcass first and then the door – wrong! It does work, but is difficult. On paper everything seems fine – but in practice a ½° out at each joint on the door stiles compounds to an unacceptable error. If you make the door first and find that it is dimensionally slightly different to the drawing it is relatively easy to alter the carcass sides to accommodate this.

Timber preparation

The first stage is to prepare the timber for the door components. I would suggest that you choose straight mild-grained stuff as this will ease the cleaning up of the door. I try to get all the parts out of one plank in order to keep a continuity of colour and grain.

The three middle stiles are cut and machined to 40 x 22mm (1½ x ⅞in) cross-section and cut to 50mm (2in) over finished length. Using a jig in a thicknesser, these are fed through to achieve the bevel (Fig 1).

As the stiles have to pass the thicknessing knives in both directions, the careful choice of timber will now be appreciated. The next stage involves passing the pieces across a surfacer,

The faceted door means that the glass shelf has to be shaped to fit

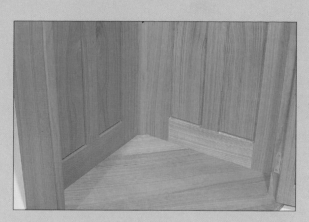

Panels are solid and book-matched in the back – note the holes for adjustable shelf fitting

The finished glazing bar joint on the door – this calls for great accuracy

(Fig 2), to form the 90° sides to the bevels. Note that the surfacer must be adequately guarded as you are passing quite small sections across.

The final stage is to machine the rebates. In the past I have done this using the dimension saw but have found that it is not accurate enough. I now use a spindle moulder with a ¼in grooving cutter (Fig 3). Again, it is imperative that the machine is properly guarded.

At the end of the brief machining exercise you will have produced the three inner stiles. As these stiles are thicker than the other door parts I handplane a small round-over on the inside edges. This makes the join a lot neater. You still need the two outer ones – but these are straightforward and with reference to the main working drawing should need no further explanation.

Rails

The next stage is to make all the rails. As can be seen from the drawings, each individual rail is rather short. I find it much easier to mark up all the rails onto two pieces of prepared timber – one for the top rails, the other for the lower. Accurate marking out is essential. Normally one chops out the mortices before cutting the tenons, but, because the top rails have an arch, this affects the width of the tenon, and therefore it is easier to have this dimension to hand before chopping the mortices.

Before cutting, it is a good idea to mark the continuity of the rails so as to avoid mixing them up later on. This is one set of tenons that will not be cut on a tenoner! There are many different ways of cutting tenons – using a carefully guarded dimension saw, a bandsaw, or even by hand. Whichever way you choose it is essential that accuracy is maintained.

Now it is time to mark and chop the mortices. I chop them using a morticer with the stile tilted over and wedged. You may find that the stile rises up when being cut – keep an eye on it. And be vigilant about the depth of cut – you wouldn't want a rectangular hole in the front face of the stile!

Glue-up

After all this fun and excitement, the next stage is to prepare for gluing up. Often I find that a cup of tea beforehand allows one to relax and think it through – it is not easy! Before any glue is applied, clean up the inside edges of all the door frames and the inside faces of the rails and stiles. From experience I now glue up these frames in parts starting with the two outside ones. Use sash cramps carefully – you will not need to use much pressure – and make sure that the cramps are kept flat during the gluing process to ensure that the frames remain flat. The centre stile and adjacent rails can also be glued (Fig 4).

Later, when gluing up the whole door I use a machine bed to lay the cramps on, to help keep the door 'flat' and out of wind. The only way I have had success with this is to lay the whole door on two sash cramps and tighten lightly, and then use G-clamps to reverse the upward tendency.

All that remains after the door has

Making sequence for glazing bar

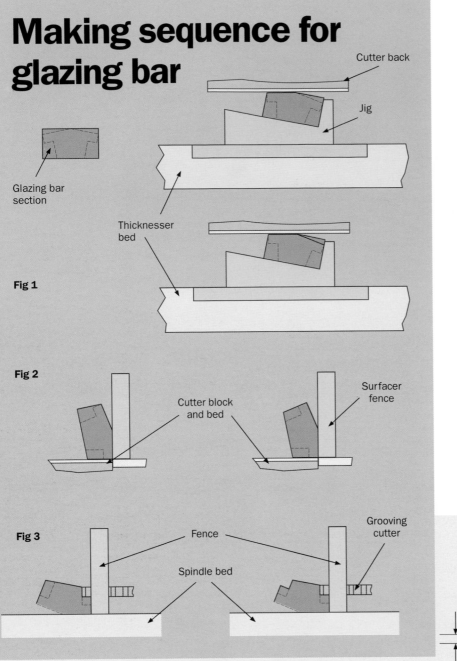

Cutter back

Jig

Glazing bar section

Thicknesser bed

Fig 1

Fig 2

Cutter block and bed

Surfacer fence

Fig 3

Fence

Spindle bed

Grooving cutter

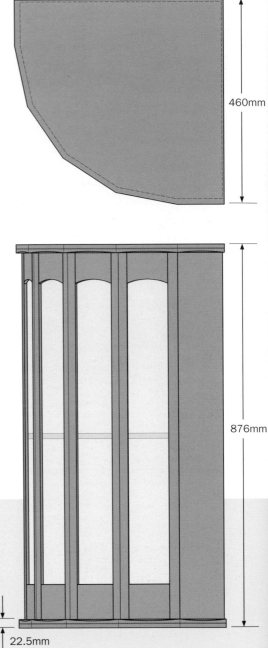

460mm

876mm

22.5mm

dried is to clean up the joint lines. This is an awkward frame to hold but I have found that supporting it on a Black & Decker workmate and using a sharp jackplane is the most successful method.

Carcass

With the door completed, you can now turn your attention to the carcass. The two frames are straightforward flat ones, each housing a pair of panels. The panels in this cabinet are deep-sawn from a thicker piece of timber to provide book-matched pairs. Use over-thick timber to give yourself a bit of play should the panels 'bend' slightly after any inherent strains are released during this process. The five carcass components are joined

to each other using 6.5mm (¼in) Finnish ply in ¼in grooves. Don't forget to mark out and drill the holes for the shelf support pegs before gluing up – it is much easier!

It is at this stage, before gluing up, that the carcass can be dry-assembled and stood on a flat surface and mated with the door. Assuming that you have paid all your bills and said your prayers, everything will fit together as you expected!

Before gluing, sand the panels to your satisfaction. I normally finish with 240-grit paper and then apply two coats of Danish oil and cut back when dry with Vaseline on 0000 wire wool. Gluing up the carcass is relatively straightforward.

When dry, carefully true the top and bottom edges and check by placing on a machine bed.

Base

The next major part is the base, which can be made in two ways. One is a solid base like the one illustrated – the other has a veneered base, which has the advantage of being more stable although it does take a lot longer.

To make the veneered base, mark out a piece of 18mm (¹¹⁄₁₆in) MDF 25mm (1in) smaller on all edges. When the edges have been cut and planed, a 6mm (¼in) groove is made around them to take a ply tongue for attaching the lipping.

The front lippings should be made

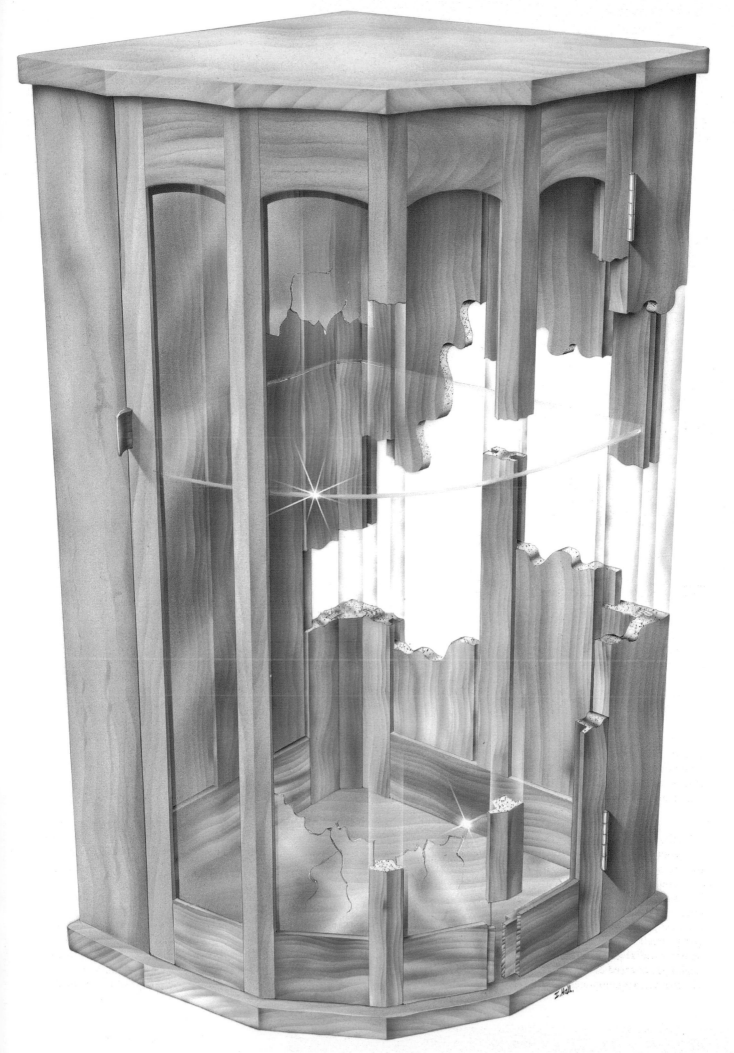

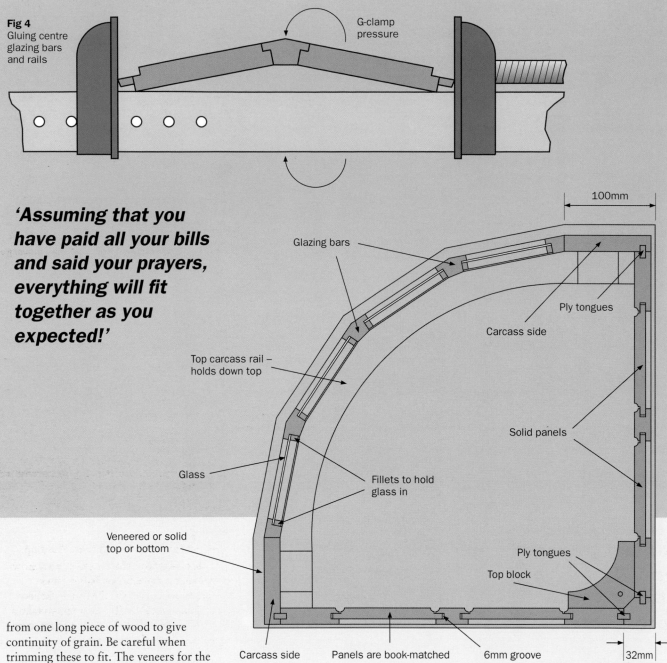

Fig 4
Gluing centre glazing bars and rails

G-clamp pressure

100mm

Glazing bars

Ply tongues

Carcass side

Top carcass rail – holds down top

Solid panels

Glass

Fillets to hold glass in

Veneered or solid top or bottom

Ply tongues

Top block

Carcass side

Panels are book-matched

6mm groove

32mm

'Assuming that you have paid all your bills and said your prayers, everything will fit together as you expected!'

from one long piece of wood to give continuity of grain. Be careful when trimming these to fit. The veneers for the top and bottom are saw-cut to 3mm (⅛in). I do this by starting off with a piece of 50mm (2in) thick timber about 75 to 100mm (3in to 4in) wide. Plane a face side and then saw off a 3mm (⅛in) thick veneer using the bandsaw. Return to the surfacer and repeat this operation until enough leaves have been cut, plus a few for luck.

Not having any clever cramping or pressing devices in my workshop, I glue these veneers with cauls and G-clamps – it is a laborious process but manageable. By using veneers this thick the resulting faces can be planed, scraped and sanded without too much worry about exposing the ground. Finish off the base by trimming the overhanging veneers and form the chamfers using a spokeshave.

Inlays

On my furniture I like to have a contrasting timber somewhere – in this case it features as two inlays, one on the top and one on the bottom. A router with a ⅟₁₆in slotting cutter is run around the six facets. I usually find it easier when working with inlays such as these to cut them over-length and cramp them to the bench at the point nearest the body.

Using a block plane, you can plane away from you to form a slight bevel with no chance of the inlay folding up and snapping. Carefully measure the length of inlay needed for each section and mitre each end as appropriate. Apply a little glue to the faces and tap in with a

pin hammer. By the time you have reached the end you can return to the beginning and clean up again using a block plane.

Base to carcass

To attach the base to the carcass I use modern coarse-thread screws in counter-bored holes which are then plugged with some similarly grained timber.

The rail at the top of the carcass, which holds the carcass firm and holds down the top, is cut from one piece of timber – if you can find a naturally curving piece, so much the better. As it is attached to the carcass sides with screws it can be slid down the inside of the

Inside of the door. The glass is held in with fillets – a fiddly fitting job!

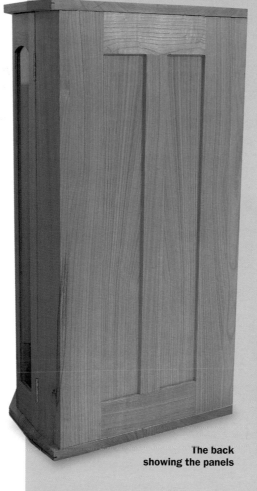

The back showing the panels

A sister cabinet of the same design in wenge

Details are noticed by clients and need careful thought and work

Cabinet upside down showing top carcass rail and fixing block

'Not having any clever cramping or pressing devices in my workshop, I glue these veneers with cauls and G-clamps – it is a laborious process but manageable'

carcass to check for parallelism. Before it is attached, the screw holes to hold the top are marked out and drilled. As a solid top will be used, slightly elongate the holes to accommodate top movement. Also needed is the hole for the magnetic catch, in this case a neat little number from Hafele. The simple block at the top rear of the cabinet which holds down the rear part of the top is simply fixed with a couple of screws.

Top

The final component is the top. Making this should not present any great headaches. To joint mine I use stopped grooves with ply insets – try not to have a visible joint line along the front edge, and use quarter-sawn stuff for the top.

On one I made, I used crown-cut boards. Attending an exhibition in a marquee one morning after a damp night, the top had dipped and had trapped the door shut – it took a while before it returned to its intended position. The top is fixed with 1¼ in x 8 brass countersunk screws.

Door hanging

The last major part is to hang the door. Assuming that all is well with the dimensions, the door should fit quite snugly into the aperture. Cutting the hinge recesses is interesting. I used a router as this is a lot gentler than a mallet and chisel. Holding the frame can be a problem. Fortunately my bench does not have any obstacles below the top and therefore it can be held quite securely

with the vice and an additional cramp.

The fillets to hold the glass in are now made and the holes drilled to allow screws to fix them to the frame. Believe me, this part is fiddly – it seems to take a whole afternoon to fit all the fillets, even with an angled-drive drill.

Finishing

I use 3mm (⅛in) glass in the doors. If you can find a glazier who can cut accurately, hang on to him – there appears to be very few around! 6mm (¼in) glass is used for the shelf with all the edges polished and chamfered. The shelf is supported with shaped blocks.

I always tend to leave handles until last. I prefer the gradual realisation of what the handle should be like whilst I am making the piece. Although it looks simple, this must be done carefully as it is the one part people tend to inspect the most.

The whole cabinet is finished with Danish oil and then 'polished' with Vaseline – I prefer the subtle sheen. ∎

A vague request for 'something in oak' inspired **Mark Constanduros** to make this glazed-oak sideboard

Mark Constanduros has been making furniture since the age of 10 and received his first commission at the age of 15. He completed a two-year design/making course at Rycotewood College, Oxfordshire, followed by a one-year BADA Furniture Restoration course at West Dean, Chichester. Mark started his own business in 1994 and shares a workshop with two other makers

Traditional in style to suit the customer, but tailored to suit the maker, too

Heart of

One of the best requests a customer can make is, 'I would like a piece of furniture to go here, but I am not sure what'. This type of question can give you the perfect opportunity to design and make anything you wish, in this case a glazed-oak sideboard.

The only stipulation was the timber, which had to be oak to go with everything else that I had made for them over the years. I had also discovered some small burrs of elm which I had veneered up some years ago and were stashed in a drawer. The perfect chance had finally arrived to incorporate them into this piece of furniture.

The basic idea was to make a traditional style of cabinet but give it a modern feel It was decided to have

leaded-light glazed doors and a burr elm frieze with a bracket foot plinth. To add a bit more character, fluted columns were added to give it a more muscular feel.

Carcass

The first job is to machine up the timber for the carcass, and start gluing up the sides, divisions and floor. Next step is to groove the front edges of the sides and divisions and the pillars (which will be tongued together with a 6mm (¼in) birch-faced ply), followed by rebating the sides to accommodate the back. The first joint has now loomed, to cut the housing in the sides for the floor. Using a fence, generally a long piece of MDF cramped to the work, and a packer you slide the router along, cutting the groove, then

remove the packer to do the last cut. With this done you can now cut out the corner of the floor to allow for the pillar to slot in place.

The cabinet divisions can be fixed in two ways. Housed and screwed or biscuit and screwed. The choice is yours. Just remember if you house it to allow for the depth when you trim the divisions to length. Both ways will need to be screwed as the downward pressure will be trying to force the joint apart. Cutting the housing is the same as before.

Top rails

With all the sides and rails trimmed to length and jointed you can now deal with the top rails, by dovetailing the ends front and back. If you step the dovetail

Above **Routing the housings for the carcass sides**
Below **Front and back rails are dovetailed into carcass sides, set back to allow fluted front columns to be planted on**

Burr elm veneers add some extra interest to the top half of the cabinet

oak

back a bit it will give you a bit more meat, making the joint slightly stronger, as the groove for jointing the pillar is quite close. The rail is then housed into the middle divisions where the rail will simply be screwed in place. You may also like to screw the dovetail in place as when the top is fitted it will try to pull the rail out. The dovetail itself is holding the sides together.

The complete carcass is now together and you can flute the columns using a 6.4mm cove bit in the router. The basic idea is that the middle flute is in the centre of the column with one either side, about 6mm (¼in) apart.

You will need to make a jig basically from bits of MDF. First, make a base and screw a stop each end to hold the pillar

in place. Having already marked out where the flutes are to stop on the pillars (running between the rails of the doors), you can measure from the outer edge of the cutter to the outer edge of the base plate of the router and screw another stop in place on both ends. By doing this you will stop in exactly the same place every time on the columns. If you do the end columns first, as they are the longest, you can then slot in the division columns and place another stop to hold these in position, remembering to always place the columns at the top of the jig. With the jig all set up, away you can go.

All the main components for the carcass are now made. Sand up the inside faces of the carcass sides and floor. These can now be dry-cramped together. With

the main carcass assembled and the rails fixed in place you can drill the holes for the adjustable shelving. The reason for carrying on making the cabinet and leaving it all cramped up in the dry is for staining, which comes at the end. If you don't want to stain it then glue it all up!

I use small brass studs, about 5mm (¼in) in diameter, which are unobtrusive but do the job more than adequately. Again, make a simple jig from an offcut of MDF. Cut this to the internal length of the cabinet side and about 80mm (3⅛in) wide and then mark out your holes about 50mm (2in) apart. There is no need to go right from the bottom to the top, but put in as many as you like, and step them in about 50mm (2in) from the edge. Mark on the jig which is the top and bottom

Veneering

Firstly, the burr elm. This involves veneering, which can be done in different ways. There are bag presses which use a compressor to suck out the air of a rubber/plastic bag creating pressure forcing the veneer onto your core (plywood). There is also hand veneering with a veneer hammer. This was how it was done in the old days, with animal glue, time-consuming and a pain in the 'wotsit'! The other way is how I did this. As the job is very small I cramped it all between the edge of my bench and a sturdy piece of oak!

Right, the core is generally plywood, and must be backed to balance out the tension. If you veneer just one side then the piece of wood you are veneering would curl. So by backing it with the same thickness as the veneer you balance out the tension keeping the piece flat.

The burr elm needs to be butt jointed and book-matched to create the pattern. Keeping the pile of veneer in order, find the middle and open it like a book, (mark these two as the centres) then do the same again with each of the halves though the second opening is upside-down, then the third opening is up the right way. With all the veneer now laid out you will need to join them all together with a nice clean butt joint. Being burr, this can be difficult as it tends to break out. I used a fresh blade on the table saw and an MDF jig to give the veneer full support through the cut. The other way is on a sanding disk, as long as it is at right-angles, otherwise you will still end up with a gap between the veneers. With them all trimmed up hold them together with veneer tape or masking tape. Mark the centre on your plywood core and take half of the veneers and glue down, tape in place so they don't slide around when sandwiching these between your blocks and cramp using G-cramps. When these have dried do the same with the other half and then glue the backing on which in this case was a piece of oak of the same thickness. In reality you should try and put the backing on at the same time as the veneer but in this case it isn't practical.

Do the same with the sides of the frame but these you could do all in one. When they are all veneered up trim them to width.

Routing the fluting for the front columns

Rails are notched and screwed to interior divisions

Ply tongue and groove for the fluted front columns

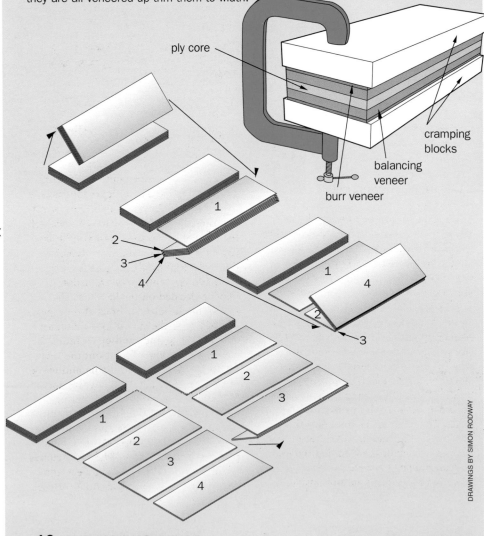

ply core

cramping blocks

balancing veneer

burr veneer

and which is the front edge. You will now know which way round to put it each time you drill the holes and know they will line up. When it comes to the divisions, you will want to stagger the holes otherwise you will end up drilling right through the carcass side into the holes on the opposite side. The jig should be set up for this as the strip of MDF is only 80mm (3⅛in) wide, so if you flip the jig it will offset the holes by 25mm (1in). After all the holes are drilled just go round with the countersink bit – just a touch on each one to clean off the whiskers. It also neatens them up.

The next step is the really interesting part – making the top. This is made up

DRAWINGS BY SIMON RODWAY

> **'I used a fresh blade on the table saw and an MDF jig to give the veneer full support through the cut'**

solid top

ply core

frame screwed through to top

burr veneer

biscuit-jointed mitres

dovetailed rail

floor housing

mortice and tenon

glass beading

ply tongue

plinth biscuited

tongue-and-groove back

in many components, the top frame and underframe. The top is basically your chosen pieces of oak glued together with a moulding. The frame is the burr elm and the underframe is what will hold the top section to the carcass.

Top frame

While the veneers have been gluing you can make the underframe, which has a 10mm (⅜in) bull-nose on the edge and a rebate for the veneered frame to locate on. Mitre the corners and joint together with biscuits. The underframe should be wide enough so that you have something to screw into when it is fixed to the carcass. Lay the glued frame onto the carcass and trim the back to length.

Before mitring the veneered frame, veneer the end of the frame sides that are at the back as it doesn't look too good having a bit of plywood showing. Now mitre them to fit and glue on the rebate.

Next step is to fit a back rail to the frame which can be screwed and glue-blocked in place to give the top something to be screwed to.

With the moulding of your choice on the top, lay it upside down and position the completed underframe. The top should be wider to allow for an overhang at the back, and for the skirting board. To fix the top at the front just use biscuits. To get their location use a strip of MDF and screw to the top against the back edge of the frame and mark the biscuit locations. The sides and back are just screwed but slotted to allow for the top to expand and contract. You can glue the front edge but not the sides or the back.

The backboards, 12mm (½in) thick, are just tongue-and-grooved but in this case have a small bead on their edges. As the cabinet is glazed it adds a bit more interest when you look inside.

Plinth

Making the plinth is again a job for another jig. The bracket foot is very traditional and probably the nicest feature for a plinth. Due to the depth of the cabinet the bracket foot would have to be very small on the sides, which I don't feel looks right, so just leave it solid and concentrate on the front. Having decided on the height of the plinth, mark out your bracket on a piece of MDF to make sure it looks the part, then cut it out and sand up so the curves are smooth. To cut out the real plinth lay the wood on the jig and mark out the pattern, cut off the waste and trim up with a router and a bearing-guided cutter. To join the ends up cut out the waste on the bandsaw and either trim up using the router or use a hand plane to finish the job. Where the curves of the foot meet the straight clean the corner up to a right angle using a chisel.

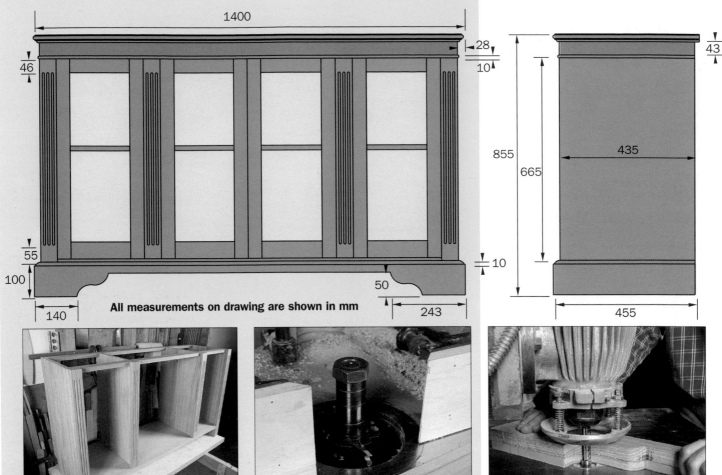

1400

46

28
10

855

665

435

43

55

100

50

140

All measurements on drawing are shown in mm

243

10

10

455

Completed main carcass, dry-assembled

The top carcass frame that supports the burr elm veneered pieces is rebated on the spindle

Profiling the plinth brackets on the overhead router

A small moulding is then routed onto the top of the plinth. With this done you can mitre the joints and fix to the carcass with blocks screwed and glued.

Doors

The doors are all morticed and tenoned and I have to admit to cheating when it comes to the rebate for the leaded-light windows. You should do stepped shoulder mortices and tenons but I just do the normal tenon and then rout out the rebate. The leaded lights are then held in place with a bead which is mitred at the corners and screwed in place.

(Stepped shoulder mortices and tenons are a pain and I avoid them!)

The doors are all trimmed to fit and hinged, then the catches can be fitted. In this case I used magnetics which generally I am not a fan of but they were the only suitable ones for this job as the doors closed onto a rail.

The whole cabinet is now made but not glued together! Scarey! Dismantle the whole cabinet, numbering the joints, and with masking tape mask off the

areas that need to be glued. It's now staining time; admittedly the cabinet looks good in the natural but it's the customers that are living with it and they want it stained, so here goes. I use a Nitrostain which is spirit-based and comes in a variety of shades. Using a rag, spread evenly, but don't overdo the quantity as it generally bleeds. By the way, the stain is fairly smelly so wear a mask or use in a ventilated area.

When everything is stained, glue it all up, remembering to make sure that the cabinet is square, otherwise the doors will not fit properly. Apply the finish of your choice – in this case it was a fine-sprayed satin lacquer. Fix the glass in, hang the doors and then fix the handles.

The handles I use are reproduction antique brass from a company called Marshall Brass. They are lovely handles of a decent weight and look good. You can get them polished, as these are, or antiqued. They offer a full service and have a very good selection. I get all my handles from them. Worth giving them a shout if you want quality. ∎

Back of the cabinet, veneered framework with the tongue-and-groove panels

Further information

For details of handles by Marshall Brass, please contact the firm on Tel: 01362 684105 Fax: 01362 684280.

Mike Cowie turned to cabinetmaking after being made redundant. He took a City & Guilds course at Sheffield College which he passed with distinction, set up his own workshop, and is now in the happy position of having as much work as he can cope with.

PHOTOGRAPHS BY STEPHEN HEPWORTH

Pale and interesting – if not overdone, liming can be an attractive finish

Quick on the drawer

Mike Cowie describes a limed chest of drawers he made at breakneck speed at college

This limed chest is one of the many items I made while attending Sheffield College on a furniture-making course. It is a frame and panel chest of drawers with a limed finish.

The carrot that had me working so avidly was the prospect of actually earning my living from my new craft, however at this time it was still some way off, hence my attempts to cram as much knowledge in as possible. Rather than, as is more the norm, committing to a major project in the second year of the course, I elected to build as many different pieces as possible to build up a practical working knowledge to supplement the theoretical side. That, at least, was the idea and mostly proved successful, however when learning new skills there are always the trials and tribulations to counterbalance the successes.

Part of the learning process was in identifying the cusp of success or failure – the point when a situation descends into hopelessness. This is usually through overworking a piece, with experience being the determining factor. Experience,

of course, creates that inner voice that learns from having grown tired of making the same mistake repeatedly and yells caution! It's up to the individual whether they choose to listen.

Judging by eye

On to the chest. I had an idea in mind of what I was aiming for. Generally, I dispense with plans and cutting lists – which sounds anarchic, but something had to give. It is surprising how efficient the eye can be in judging and estimating, particularly when a project involves expensive timber.

For the legs I cut eight pieces planed to 20mm (¾in) thick by 70mm (2¾in) wide, left slightly long in length. These were then identified as to position, front, side and so on, with mortices marked – one first then all the others from this, all mortices being alike. The mortices were all cut on an industrial morticer, which is excellent; however, returning home from using the college's machines is another matter!

Having completed all the mortices the

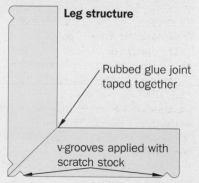

Top is lipped and moulded and the legs are made up into an L-section

Leg structure

Rubbed glue joint taped together

v-grooves applied with scratch stock

Timber tips

From an early stage I have adopted a policy of purchasing as much timber as my budget allows, which is never as much as I would like. This I regard as an investment. Then rightly or wrongly I immediately plane the timber up to the maximum thickness it will bear – I have been known to use the machine shop at Sheffield College, to the continuing despair of Pete Brown, the tutor!

I then leave this timber to rest under its own weight in store, without stickers, where some pieces may reign for years. This system seems to work very well, allowing me to match my timber to projects easily, while it takes up less space in store and is easier to handle than raw timber. I always hope this system allows some of the stresses to subside within the wood.

With a current stock of around 140cu.ft, I have a working knowledge of each board, which helps enormously to speed up work and reduce waste – but then I go and ruin it all by pulling every single one of the boards that may fit, spending time deciding!

'. . . I will continue to employ the table saw to rough out, with the router to finish my tenons'

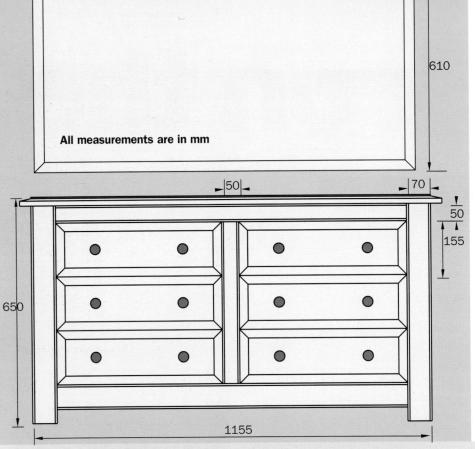

All measurements are in mm

End panels are made of ash

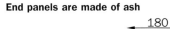

table saw is then angled to 45°. A test piece ensures accuracy. For the glue-up I found that a rubbed joint with Sellotape holding the mitres together proved adequate. I put it aside to set. Rails for the front, back and sides, together with muntins, were all thicknessed and cut to size, mortices for the muntins marked and cut. Next, the tenons could be cut, on a single-headed tenoner. These machines are definitely aspirational for the furniture-maker, though very expensive. Until the day comes when I obtain one I will continue to employ the table saw to rough out, with the router to finish my tenons. A trial fit was

beneficial at this point, to help identify any problems, adjust accordingly, and to help decide which was to be the front and back; a large knot made the decision easy for me. Now the back and sides required grooving for the panels. I drew a pencil line on to identify which edge was which. The groove, 4mm (^{5}⁄₃₂in), was machined with the spindle moulder; however, as I am well aware, the router is perfectly able to handle such tasks, if a little noisily.

At this stage I considered placement of the drawer runners and kickers. I found sycamore (because I had some on hand) excellent for this purpose.

There are three equal-sized drawers on each side, so I subdivided the legs and marked for double mortices on the inside of front and back legs. When marked I used one of the legs to transfer the same marks to both muntins to ensure accuracy. I cut the mortices. If I had been using the router to cut mortices, this stage would have featured alongside cutting the rail mortices.

Runners

So, on to the runners. I took sycamore, planed to thickness and cut to length, then cut twin-stub tenons on the bandsaw, setting the fence for multiple

ILLUSTRATIONS BY SIMON RODWAY

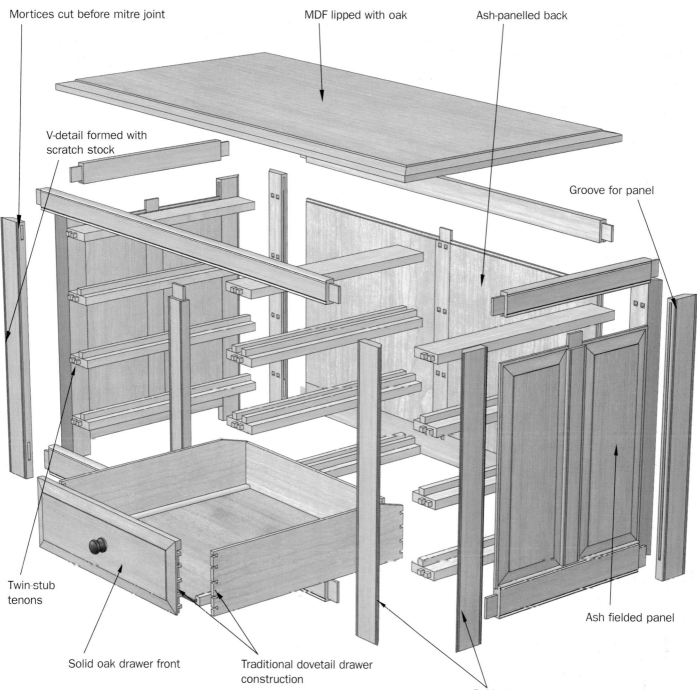

Mortices cut before mitre joint

MDF lipped with oak

Ash-panelled back

V-detail formed with scratch stock

Groove for panel

Twin-stub tenons

Solid oak drawer front

Traditional dovetail drawer construction

Rubbed and mitred joint

Ash fielded panel

cuts and chopping out by hand. I made the runners broad enough to accommodate the drawer adequately. Prior to gluing up, I used a scratch stock to form a small moulding along the edges. I used native ash for the panels. I find an oak and ash mix well balanced – of course it had nothing at all to do with the fact that I already had some ash shorts and narrows in stock! I planed them up to 20mm (¾in) thickness and jointed them to form the necessary width, then I trimmed them to size and profiled them on the spindle moulder, with a relief cut on the back until I achieved a nice fit. I left 100mm (4in) for a degree of

expansion. I finished the panels with Danish oil – to my regret, for it was at this time I discovered Danish oil yellows ash unduly. Now I much prefer a white polish, instead.

I did the glue-up in stages, with the sides first, then muntins, panels, legs and runners. I checked them for square and left them to set. Rails and back panels were added later to finish the carcass. Drawer guides were required, being cut to length and glued in place using a straight edge to locate them correctly. The top was constructed from 18mm MDF, lipped with oak, mitred at the corners and veneered. I achieved the

veneering with the aid of a huge mechanical veneer press, which does make life easy, and while I am informed vacuum bag presses work effectively, I have yet to countenance the high cost. In the meantime I use an old 40mm (1½in) worktop with an array of clamps and bearers. After veneering, the edge was moulded in the same manner as the panels and fixed in place with metal L-plates, although left off for the moment.

Finishing

I chose lime for the finish, though only on the oak. Reading up on the process, I was advised to open the grain with a

Back panels always look good in solid wood – here they are also made in ash

Drawers

My very first drawer was something of a mongrel, because in my haste, being unprepared to wait in the queue for the machines, I decided to construct the drawer prior to finishing the carcass. If nothing else, it brought a wry smile to the face of Malcolm, the tutor – I still think he could have warned me, though! In the end I managed to obtain a decent fit with the addition of two slips glued on the sides. However, it did serve as an important lesson, something I now always consider when starting on drawers.

There was a time when I considered dovetails as the epitome of craftsmanship, something that would only come with time and plenty of practice, which needed a dovetail jig to enable a maker to construct these difficult joints with a degree of professionalism. Not a bit of it! The only secret of quality dovetails, as indeed anything else, is correct attention to detail and using the right tool for the job. Eventually I dispensed with the jig, finding it too noisy and fiddly to set up, with its mechanical-looking joints. The moral here is never underestimate your own abilities – give yourself a fair chance before marching off to the toolshop for the latest gimmick.

The drawer fronts were selected (from dwindling stock), planed to size and cut to fit the openings with a little left on the depth to plane to fit later. Drawer sides and backs were sycamore, deep cut on the bandsaw, finishing at 8mm (½in) on the thicknesser, planed to width and all cut to length. As for the dovetails, I was aiming for pins that

were as narrow as possible, for a saw kerf thickness. Well, all you can do is try! As for cutting the tails out I found no fault with the bandsaw, stopping just short of the line, being aware of the bandsaw's tendency to run on. Dovetails chopped out, I attempted a partial fit, similar for the back. Due to the thickness of the sides, drawer slips were employed, with the router used to groove the front. I cleaned up the insides of the drawers, assembled them, checked them for square and left them on one side to set. I glued drawer slips in place with the bottoms cut to size – unfortunately funds didn't run to cedar of Lebanon, so instead I used 6mm (¼in) plywood. As this piece was to be for our own use it didn't really matter. However, there is no substitute for cedar, which gives a lovely aroma when the drawer is opened. The drawers were planed to fit and sanded, bottoms screwed in place, with the drawer runners doubling as a drawer stop.

Detailing on drawer front

> **'There was a time when I considered dovetails as the epitome of craftsmanship, something that would only come with time and plenty of practice'**

stiff brush, then apply the lime paste with hessian cloth, rubbing across the grain – none of which I found helpful! Oak has an open grain, hessian is too absorbent for the paste, and rubbing across the grain left it streaky. Instead, I used cotton cloth, rubbed with the grain, which proved a little more successful, though it required a little practice, which of course could account for the primer! All of the oak was limed with water-based lacquer selected to fix it in place – the lacquer, being water-based, raises the grain, so I rubbed it down carefully to avoid removing all the lime, and applied a further two coats.

Nice chest – shame about the handles! Expediency is my only excuse – no other handles were available and I was reluctant to find the time to turn any. Brass handles, purchased at a bankruptcy sale, were fitted as a temporary fix and there they have remained. The chest lives in my son's room; however, as he is preparing to go to university I may just find the time to make some wooden ones. ∎

Mike Cowie turned to cabinetmaking after being made redundant. After passing with distinction a City & Guilds course at Sheffield, he set up his own workshop and is now in the happy position of having as much work as he can cope with

PHOTOGRAPHY BY STEPHEN HEPWORTH

Mike Cowie begins making a kitchen dresser with angled legs and burr

A traditional farmhouse kitchen wood, elm can have an almost exotic richness to it

Groovy dresser

The first point of contact with a new customer is usually via a phone call, and so it proved for this job. These clients had taken my card at a small display that I had attended – which just goes to show the benefit to be had in getting out and about.

They were after something to fill a wall in a redecorated kitchen, the choice being wide open for both style and materials. Apart from kitchen cabinets which were to be painted, there was as yet no other furniture.

The intention was to create a slightly rustic look, something more befitting a kitchen than living room, something functional, pleasing to look at, and well made at a reasonable price.

Of course, the clients determine whether I succeed or fail, and in this case they were happy with my ideas for the proposed dresser, presented in my usual fashion as a sketch. I prefer, if possible, to work with a degree of discretion as there never seems to be time to sit down and do detailed drawings. A computer with a CAD program might help but would I ever get the chance to learn how to use it?

Working this way, I find my enjoyment of producing is enhanced because I'm able to incorporate ideas into the piece while building it. I suggested making the dresser in oak (*Quercus robur*) and elm (*Ulmus* spp), thinking these would complement one another. When my clients came to view timbers they opted for the elm, a good choice, I think, as elm has a lively quality, with a depth not found in other timbers.

They also wanted some colour and slight burr incorporated into the unit.

That was the worst part over. One day I will feel at ease when dealing with clients. For the moment, I have to learn

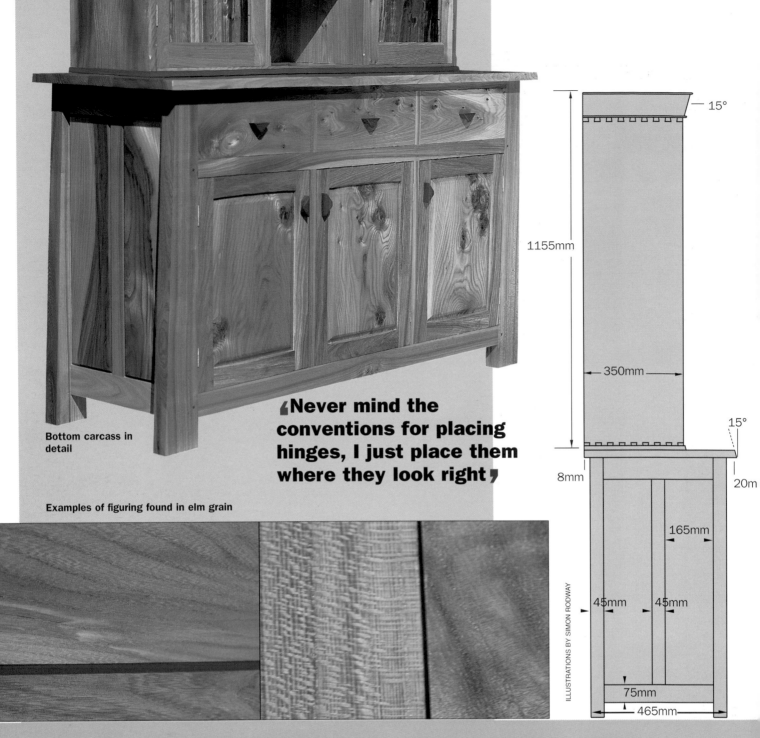

Bottom carcass in detail

Examples of figuring found in elm grain

> "**Never mind the conventions for placing hinges, I just place them where they look right**"

1155mm

350mm

8mm

15°

15°

20m

165mm

45mm

45mm

75mm

465mm

ILLUSTRATIONS BY SIMON RODWAY

to relax and take it easy. But with three, four and even five jobs on the go at one time this is hard. It's a funny old world, if I had no work I'd only fret . . .

Preparation

I like when possible to build up a store of timber. It may be fanciful on my part but I prefer to plane to as thick as possible and lay down under weights, believing that the stresses might be relieved somewhat. Either that or I just like to hoard the stuff. With such a small workshop I know all the wood intimately. The timber used in this project had been in store for over two years.

Legs

As ever on a new job I was itching to get started – and where better than on

the legs? They are made from 50mm (2in) elm, and all four legs are cut from the same quarter-sawn slab of wood, using the sloping side to avoid having too much waste.

The angled legs are the main feature of the bottom unit, the wood being allowed to speak for itself for the rest. The legs are planed up keeping them as thick as possible, left slightly overlong for any possible revision, and marked for mortices. One acts as a template for the rest.

Using the router for morticing, which is my preferred method when possible, the mortices are cut out, the ends squared up with a chisel – a curiously pleasant chore after the noise of the router, the relaxing tap of mallet on chisel being quite soothing.

Rails

Mortices are cut for the inside rails at the same time. The rails are also cut from the straight-grained wood – a personal preference here as I feel that using straight-grained wood for the carcass allows a showcase for the doors and drawers.

All six rails, three front and three back, are cut to length together, scribed with a marking gauge and tenoned or, in the case of the top two rails, dovetailed.

Tenons are cut on the bandsaw, the rails being a little too long for the table saw, and finished off with the router for a nice clean fit. The shoulders are handsawn and pared back to the scribed line with a chisel – an obvious contradiction here for one who professes

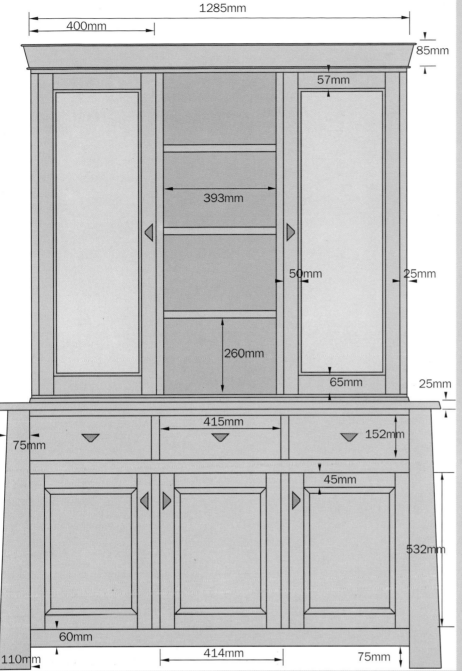

'The shoulders are handsawn and pared back to the scribed line with a chisel – an obvious contradiction here for one who professes always to look for the quickest method'

Drawer enclosure and stop

Quarter-sawn oak sides

always to look for the quickest method.

The same applies to the side rails.

Trial assembly

A trial assembly enables a measure to be taken for the side muntins and front door stiles. This is also an opportune time to mark out and cut in the dovetails for the top rails.

Cut the mortices for the muntins while the front is divided into three equal sections. Fit the door stiles with double tenons to complete the base carcass.

Select some coloured elm, plane it and cut it to size, allowing 5mm (³⁄₁₆in) on each edge. Cut grooves in the carcass to 6mm (¼in) to accommodate the panels.

The fielded panels are produced using a cove cutter in the router. Finish them by using a rebate cutter on the back until

they fit snugly in their recesses.

The back and bottom panels are in plywood, grooved and rebated for the back so that it can be glued in place to act as a strengthener.

The bottom is fitted onto a support which, in turn, is glued into a groove cut with the router.

Clean up the carcass prior to gluing, planing any high spots, scraping where necessary and sanding everywhere.

Hinges, runners

Using the router – much faster than by hand – cut in the hinges. This task is always better attempted before the glue-up. Never mind the conventions for placing hinges, I just place them where they look right.

Mark the positions with a sharp knife

and square off, set a marking gauge to the width and cut the back line in. Setting the router fence to this line, adjust to the required depth of cut and rout away. Square up the ends with a chisel to enable six hinges to be cut in minutes to precise depth.

Door hinges are worked directly from these and again cut with the router.

Add the drawer runners, morticed and tenoned into the rails.

Carcass glue-up

Glue up the front and back, keeping a check on square. Add the sides and drawer runners when the front and back are dry, and leave to set. Choose straight-grained timber for the door frames. These are morticed and tenoned and grooved for the panels, using the router.

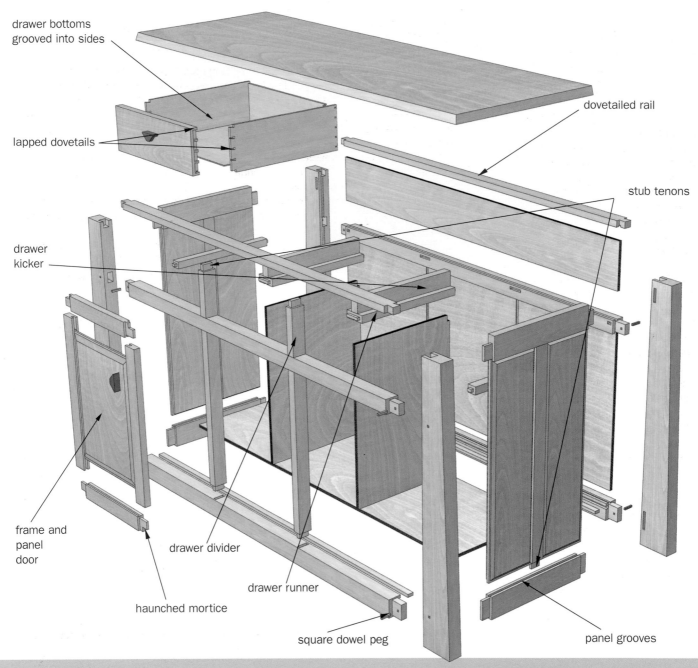

drawer bottoms grooved into sides

lapped dovetails

dovetailed rail

stub tenons

drawer kicker

drawer divider

frame and panel door

haunched mortice

drawer runner

square dowel peg

panel grooves

There's no need to construct an elaborate jig. Simply plane another piece of timber to the same thickness as the workpiece, then clamp the workpiece to it or, even better, place it in a bench vice. This gives a stable platform from which to work, particularly when morticing near to the end of the timber. Two of the workpieces end-butted together, with the scrap acting as a fence, solve the problem of the router dipping at the end.

Drawers, interior

Normally I prefer thin drawer sides, but for this job I opted for quarter-sawn oak for the sides and back, thinking that thicker was more in order – nice and robust. It will come as no surprise to learn that I used dovetails (see panel *I'd know the difference*, above).

A nice piece of wood was chosen for the drawer fronts, although I was initially hesitant for there was a large live knot at one end. Fearing that this may prove awkward to joint, so ruining all the fronts, nevertheless I proceeded with this and fortunately, with a little care, proved successful.

Due to the thickness of the drawer sides, grooves are cut directly into the cedar of Lebanon (*Cedrus libani*) bottoms. Glue these together, leave them to set, then tidy up, planing to fit. Fill the drawer stops and fit the handles.

Place two dividers on the inside and glue them up into grooves cut on the inside of the door stiles. Screw into place from the rear, then add a shelf in the central section.

Finishing

Select, plane and butt-joint timber for the top to achieve a close fit.

Then all that is needed is a quick skim over with the belt sander fitted with a new 120-grit belt. Remove grit marks with scrapers and finish off with the orbital sander.

Using a power saw set at an angle, trim the edges of the top with the front cut on the plane.

Allow up to a week for the oiling process, and remove all loose items, like doors and shelves.

Proceed by applying one coat, leaving to set, rubbing down and reapplying daily. I could so easily be tempted to spray – and an apprentice would be better still . . .

Next: the upper section.

I'd know the difference

A good client once questioned the need for hand-cut dovetails, asking bluntly: 'Who would know the difference?'

I found this quite disheartening for when we enter the craft is it not the dovetail to which we all aspire? I'm thinking of the quality, clean, crisply cut dovetail that, on delivering the piece to the client, we can dwell upon, opening the drawers to display it proudly. Or am I beginning to take this too seriously? Should I be listening to that little warning voice at the back of my mind which usually keeps me in check by whispering 'anorak'?

While I'm aware of the modern business 'pile it high, sell it cheap' policies that are affecting towns and cities, in reality it is only the reasonably well heeled who are willing and able to purchase our goods. Therefore we have to strive to ensure that the spirit of the old craftsmen lives on.

I take a fairly liberal interpretation of hand-cutting dovetails. In reality I cut the tails out on the bandsaw, relieving most of the waste with the router. Being pragmatic – and honest – if I could price my work for complete handwork I would be a happy man!

Panels and chamfers

The panels had been selected earlier from some partially burred boards, cut to size and thickness. I didn't have a suitable cutter to accomplish my intended fielding pattern, but utilising a panel cutter at partial depth achieved the desired result.

When placed in the frame, the transition from the square edge to the rounded panel looked wrong, hence the spokeshaved chamfer which does, I think, enhance the overall look.

The panels are then rebated on the back to fit into the groove, cleaned up and finished with Danish oil, so that any shrinkage that might occur will not show up as unfinished wood around the edge.

Oiling takes approximately three to four days, applying one coat in the morning, rubbing it down and putting on another in the evening – at least in summer when the temperature is higher.

This should be repeated daily until you are satisfied with the result. The finished panels are glued into their frames, left to set, then planed to fit the cavity. I usually leave doors slightly oversize, planing each to fit their respective positions. ∎

Soft panels and chamfer detail. Chamfers like this are a typical feature of the Arts and Crafts movement

End panels

Creating a spokeshave chamfer

PHOTO COURTESY OF BOB WEARING

Mike Cowie turned to cabinetmaking after being made redundant. After passing with distinction a City & Guilds course at Sheffield, he set up his own workshop and is now in the happy position of having as much work as he can cope with.

The upper case

Mike Cowie finishes off the top layer of his dresser

PHOTOGRAPHS BY STEPHEN HEPWORTH

During a break to Ullswater in the Lake District I often found myself stopping to admire the wonderfully healthy trees. Sadly, I never did get round to finding a timber yard from which to purchase some lakeland wood. And my situation was becoming desperate, as making the upper section of the dresser would leave my limited stock of elm (*Ulmus procera*) in serious need of replenishing.

Upper section

The lower section complete, timber was planed for the upper. The length was decided by standing the uprights in place, adjusting them until they appeared to fit, measurements were taken and the top and bottom cut to length. The depth was kept to 305mm (12in) in order to allow sufficient space for both display and storage.

The corner joints were lapped dovetails for strength, the hardest part being balancing the long sides while marking the pins. Care was taken when attempting to match the wood with top, bottom and inner uprights from the same planks with the outer from the same batch as the top of the lower case.

The uprights were cut to length and fitted into housings cut with the router using a simple guide jig, and the ends of the uprights were rebated to fit. A rebate was also cut to accommodate the back panel. As for the lower parts, the top was divided into three equal sections, the centre being left open with three fixed shelves, housed and rebated. The two outer sections were to have glass-fronted doors with adjustable shelving. This involved the fitting of brass grommets into drilled holes for

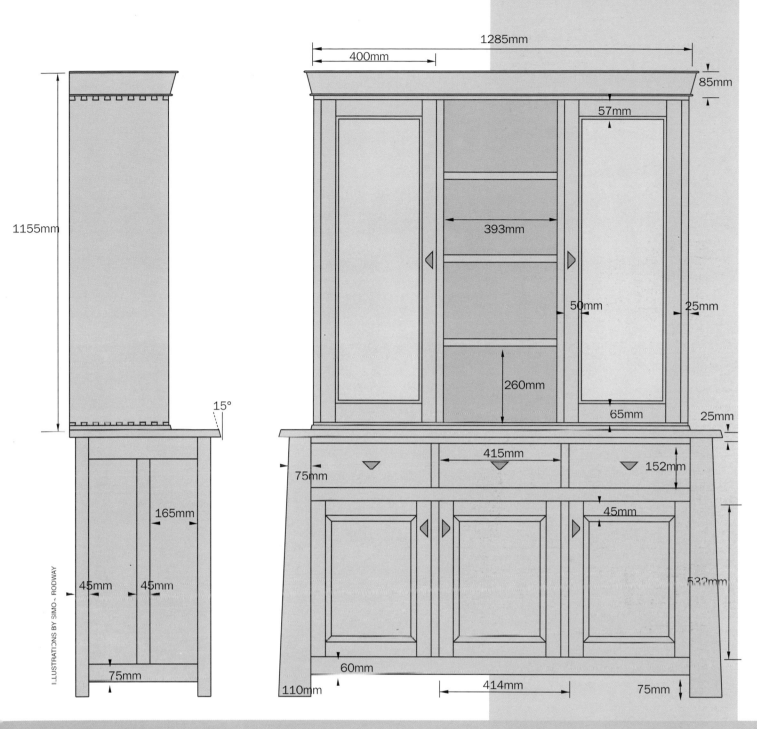

which a template was used in order to space the holes evenly – a piece of scrap wood with holes proved quite effective for this. This done, the two inner uprights and shelves were glued together and left to set. The sides, top and bottom were then cleaned up – the scraper and orbital sander being adequate for the insides and the belt sander being added for the outers. Hinges were cut in at this stage with a bevel added to the outer edges of the uprights.

This done, the outer carcass was ready for gluing together and this time I was ready for it – cramps, blocks cut and waiting, glue table set in plenty of space and even steps on hand to enable me to reach the top.

Sticking points

I applied the glue – I recall reading along the lines of, 'the old timers placed just a touch of glue on each surface'. I like to see a little squeeze out of the joint to indicate that there has been an even spread, rather than rivulets running down the job. I used to use a small brush to apply glue, but I now find the index finger more versatile and always to hand! My preparation certainly worked – if only I could apply the same principle to the rest of life.

The top having been glued together, it was now time to fit in the shelves. These could simply be slid into place, this time with only a light touch of glue, clamped and left to set.

The doors for the upper case are elm. However, bearing in mind my previous disappointments with elm, I had cut some straight-grained timber into thin sections and left it standing for two weeks to see how it would react. It reacted very well, thankfully. This was then cut to length, morticed and tenoned. With the router, I shaped a 45° bevel on the front and cut a rebate for the glass on the reverse.

Jointing at the mitres was done with a little jig, a length of timber cut at 45° at

"When fitting a cornice I like to cut a rebate along the top edge of the case so that it fits snugly and can be removed during transportation"

Top carcass – showing jarrah detail

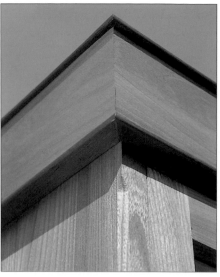

Cornice and corner of carcass – note the chamfer detail

Detail makes the difference – handles in matching jarrah

"Fortunately the wood chosen did not have much spring in it when the boards were passed through the thicknesser to clean up"

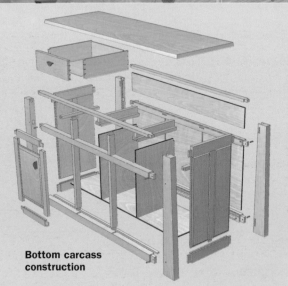

Bottom carcass construction

both ends, 100mm (4in) wide x 460mm (18in) long, with a small strip applied to the bottom on both sides. This allows the workpiece to be placed on the jig, held in the vice and a tidy mitre trimmed with a sharp chisel.

For the mortice rail I sped things up by using the router to trim off most of the waste with a small cutter. Another benefit of leaving a little extra length to the stiles is that it enables you to set the fence.

Doors were glued together and planed to fit, with the hinges cut in. When fitting a cornice I like to cut a rebate along the top edge of the case so that it fits snugly and can be removed during

> **"Meanwhile, I shall apply a couple more coats of oil and concentrate on my next major problem – how to fit it into my car!"**

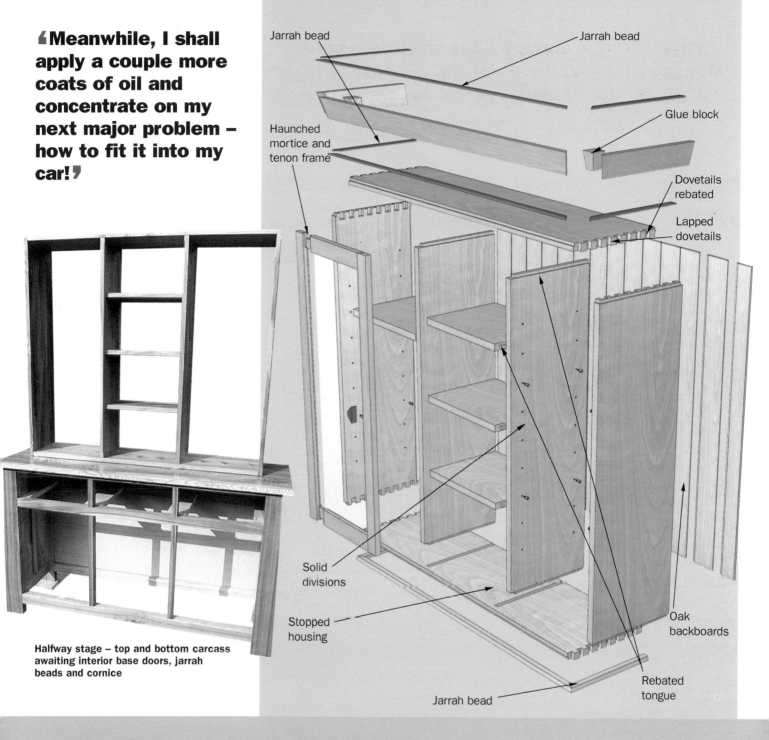

Jarrah bead

Jarrah bead

Glue block

Haunched mortice and tenon frame

Dovetails rebated

Lapped dovetails

Solid divisions

Stopped housing

Oak backboards

Jarrah bead

Rebated tongue

Halfway stage – top and bottom carcass awaiting interior base doors, jarrah beads and cornice

transportation. In common with the angles on the bottom, the cornice was mitred to this same angle and given a jarrah (*Eucalyptus marginata*) bead to sit on top, to match the handles which will be in either jarrah or padauk (*Pterocarpus* spp.).

Back-up measures

I used oak (*Quercus robur*) for the back panels as I didn't have any thin-section elm. I made a 25mm (1in) deep cut on the table saw by removing and passing the wood over a 25mm (1in) cut. This was done on both edges, gradually increasing it to the maximum cut size of 50mm

(2in). Finally, I fed it through the bandsaw – the saw kerfs acting as guides for the bandsaw blade. The maximum I can cope with is 150mm (6in) which, if I try directly on the bandsaw, always seems to wander off the line. Yes, I do have the saw set for a straight cut; however, it is in such regular use it tends to get abused, so I go for the easiest possible method.

Fortunately the wood chosen did not have much spring in it when the boards were passed through the thicknesser to clean up. These were then rebated, alternating front and back on each edge, with the back rebate being marginally smaller than the front, so that a small gap

is created as a feature on the boards.

The boards were then oiled up and fixed in place.

And finally, the glass. As plain glass did not look quite right, I chose Pilkington's 'Warwick' – a machine-produced glass with a handmade, rustic look that I felt complemented the unit. The clients agreed with my choice and I put in an order for the toughened, safety glass version.

And that just about completed the job, although I am still waiting on the delivery of the handles. Meanwhile, I shall apply a couple more coats of oil and concentrate on my next major problem – how to fit it into my car! ■

A joint venture

● ROSWITHA LENTGE and JEFF SMITH took Diplomas in Furniture Craft and Management at Buckinghamshire College, before spending some years running their own furniture design business in Devon. Now living in New Zealand, they are continuing to make furniture

Roswitha Lentge and **Jeff Smith** make an oak display cabinet

RIGHT: A modern Gothic cabinet

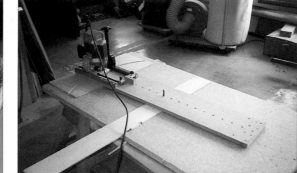

FAR LEFT: Detail
of handles

LEFT: A trammel
is used to form
the profiles of the
templates for
making the
laminating
formers

For our display cabinet we decided to use solid quarter-sawn oak (*Quercus* spp) throughout, which meant that movement considerations were to play a major part. We also decided to use brown oak as an effective contrast for the glazed bars, handles, cockbeading and drawer slips.

'The back face of the glazing bars will be grooved so that they fit snugly over the ribs'

Drawing

Start by making a full-size drawing, on 3mm MDF, of the side and front elevations.

Strict accuracy is required as you will be relying directly on the drawing for marking out and jointing.

The well-figured quarter-sawn oak and brown oak components are cut and planed oversize and then put to settle down in stick.

Door bars

We chose to laminate the identical curved bars, using three laminates of 9mm (overwidth) by 4mm (⅜ by ⅛in), the curved bars being planed down to final thickness later.

To make these laminates, plane down enough timber to 9mm (⅜in) thickness with a face edge. Rip the timber to 4mm (⅛in) laminates.

Make sure that you pencil a marking on the face so that you can

place the laminates back into their natural sequence.

To make the male and female formers, use a long beam compass to mark off the correct radii onto template material, for example 6mm MDF, which is pinned down.

From the same pivot points, set up a router trammel, cutting inside and outside radii in separate operations. These templates can then be pinned to thicker material, say 22mm MDF, and shaped on a router or spindle moulder to give the formers.

Wax the face of the formers and get going on gluing up the laminations, whilst proceeding with the rest of the job.

The back face of the glazing bars will be grooved so that they fit snugly over the ribs. Use veneers to make up the curved ribs to 3mm (⅛in) thickness by laminating them to the correct radius.

Carcass

Once the sides, top, base and fixed shelf have been planed and dimensioned to size, the top corners of the carcass are mitred and biscuited together. The mitres are cut in the sliding table saw set at 45°.

The base and fixed shelf are also biscuited to the sides. These require accurate jointing, especially as you are making a drawer aperture. Make suitable fences for the biscuit jointer to run against, which can be clamped down on the sides.

For the back, we chose to veneer 6mm MDF with crown-cut oak and a backing. Do this before running the grooves in the top and sides so that an offcut can be used to ensure a good fit.

Cornice

The large profile of the cornice is cut on a spindle moulder. The front

'Because we chose to make this piece in solid, it is vital that potential movement in the timber is taken into consideration'

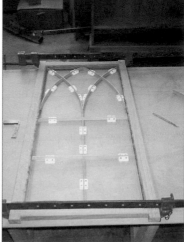

FAR LEFT: Glazing
bars and former

LEFT: Blocks
screwed to setting
out rod hold
down the ribs
while the door is
dry-assembled to
get an exact fit

cornice section is mitred accurately and biscuited to the top. A reinforcement strip is also biscuited into the top, behind this cornice section.

Timber movement

Because we chose to make this piece in solid, it is vital that potential movement in the timber is taken into consideration.

Set up a dovetail router cutter in a table and cut the female groove in the cornice. With the same cutter, set it up to shape the male strips. Using a test piece will ensure you obtain the required snug fit – it should only require gentle tapping with a wooden block and hammer. Slot-screw these strips into position onto the carcass and slide the cornice into place. A small amount of glue may be used on the mitre itself and on the dovetail groove or strip. On no account get any onto the carcass or you will be defeating the object of the exercise.

The final ovolo moulding on the cornice can then be shaped using a router fitted with a bearing-guided cutter.

'With a sharp, finely set blade, make the curvature of the sole slightly more than the actual job'

Plinth

There are six feet components – two at the front, two at the side, which are mitred into the front ones, and two at the back.

Each pair is a different width and the concave profile of these is initially cut on the table saw. The two front feet are 134 by 125 by 44mm (5⅛ by 5 by 1¾in). To cut these comfortably on the table saw, double the length and add the kerf of your table saw, for example 3mm (⅛in) so that you have a manageable timber block of 271 by 125 by 44mm (10⅝ by 5 by 1¾in).

Using a template of the curve, mark this onto the block. Pass this over the top of the saw blade, adjusting the height at each cut.

Once the feet have been curved out on the table saw, you need to smooth them out with a compass plane. With a sharp, finely set blade, make the curvature of the sole slightly more than the actual job.

Plane out the score marks of the table saw and finish off with a cabinet scraper.

While the feet are still attached in length, mark out the cut-off point and mortice them for the tenoned plinth rails. The feet can then be shaped using a jig to the correct curvature on a spindle moulder or router table.

For the plinth rails, the profile is achieved with a custom-made cutter for the spindle moulder and then tenoned to length. Cut the block in half to give the two front feet. For gluing up the two side plinths, it is easier to leave them double length and split them afterwards.

Measuring from the working drawing, cut away with a jigsaw a section from each carcass side, slightly more than the shape of the plinth. The top edge of the front plinth section is biscuited to the carcass base. The side plinth sections which mitre into the front plinth section must also take into account the crossgrain of the carcass. This can be achieved by slot-screwing from behind with roundhead screws.

The plinth is finished off by the addition of a quarter-round beading strip which is glued to the top edge of the plinth.

'It follows that because the bars are brown oak, then the moulded inner edge of the doors needs to match'

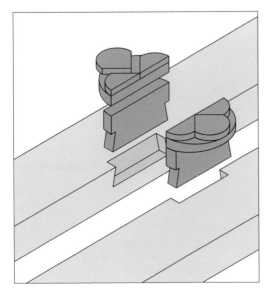

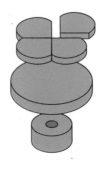

RIGHT: The back
legs are made as
one piece and
then sawn apart

FAR RIGHT: Plinth
glued together
and awaiting
biscuit jointing to
main carcass

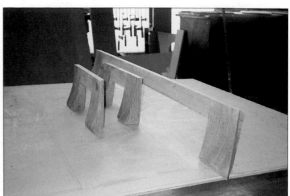

Doors

It follows that because the bars are brown oak, then the moulded inner edge of the doors needs to match. Glue on to each stile and rail, a strip of brown oak slightly thicker than the moulding. It helps to have left these components oversize at this stage so that they can now be machine-planed to size, being careful to check the thickness of the brown oak against the moulding.

The rails can now be tenoned, bearing in mind that the shoulders must extend to the bottom of the rebate in the stiles, so add this to the overall shoulder length.

Run the rebates and mouldings, making sure that the bottom of the rebate is exactly in line with the quirk, or step, on the moulding.

While the router is set up, run the same moulding on all of the bars. To mould the curved bars, set up the male former that was used to laminate them. Once this is done, change the cutter to a 3mm straight bit and again, run the grooves to the correct depth in the back of the ribs.

Ribs

A means of securing the ribs accurately in position on the drawing is required for jointing. We found it quick and convenient to use plastic 'modesty' blocks, screwed down exactly into position so that the ribs are a snug push fit. Both the straight ribs and curved ribs are glue-jointed with halving joints. The meeting point

'The meeting point where the two centre curves meet the vertical centre rib is simply butted'

where the two centre curves meet the vertical centre rib is simply butted, using epoxy resin glue.

Once the ribs are jointed, dry clamp-up the door frames, making sure they are square, and lay them in turn over the rib assembly. Line this up exactly with the drawing and mark off the shoulders from the bottom of the door rebates, using a sharp instrument such as a scalpel.

Cut the ribs to exact shoulder length. This rib assembly should now fit snugly into the door frame and will be glued in with an epoxy resin type glue.

The door stiles and frames can now be jointed to receive the bars, using the drawing to mark out their positions accurately. For the irregular angles on the top rail, we found it best to use custom-made paring jigs. The outside stiles which merge with the curved bars require careful paring, as the mitre is very acute.

Clean up the inside edges of the door components and glue them up.

Glue and assemble the rib components on top of the drawing, within the modesty blocks. Spot glue the ends of the ribs where they will butt into the glued-up door frame, which is now inserted over the top.

Check for perfect alignment over the drawing and allow to dry.

Jointing bars

Now start jointing the bars which once in place, will provide extra strength to the rib assembly. When cutting curved bars for jointing, try to use the opposing joints from the same section of material to ensure grain flow and colour match.

Remove the modesty blocks from the drawing and use this to mark off the positions of the joints on the bars. Saw these off slightly oversize.

Carefully take off the waste with the disc sander, constantly checking for final fit on the doors themselves. It helps to slightly remove some waste behind the joint to ensure it goes down well. Leave a dry fit at this stage and then glue them in altogether once each joint is fitting satisfactorily, using the epoxy resin glue.

Make sure that the bars are a snug fit, but not too tight that it causes them to bend upwards.

RIGHT: Glazing
bar make-up

FAR RIGHT: The
ends of the
carcass are cut
away behind the
plinth and slot-
screwed to allow
for movement

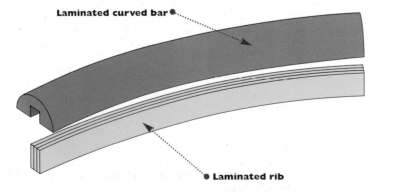

Laminated curved bar

Laminated rib

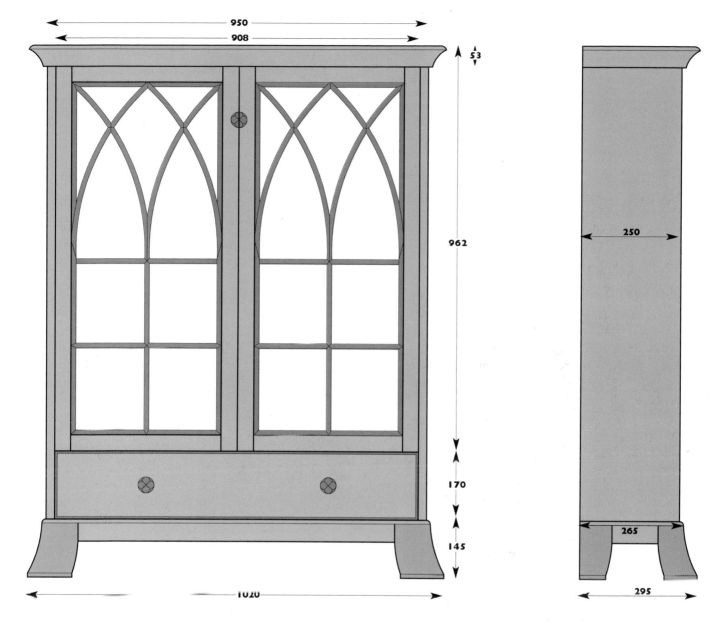

All measurements
are in millimetres

Drawer

Make and fit the drawer before hanging the doors. This drawer is cockbeaded, so remember that, in accordance to your bead size, the sides and bottom edge of the drawer front are rebated. The top edge is not usually rebated, but is reduced by the same amount, over its overall width. This takes place once the drawer has been fitted in the normal way.

As there is no shelf over the top of the drawer the front can be made to its finished width, minus the thickness of the top cockbead.

When planning your dovetails, remember to make an allowance for the thickness of the cockbead.

With rebating done, mitre and fit the narrower side and bottom beads and glue them in sparingly. The top bead being wider, it is only mitred where it meets the narrow beads on the sides. This 'part mitre' can be done by making the angled shoulder with a dovetail saw and then mitring on the guillotine, stopping short of the shoulder. Finish off by

paring down to the shoulder by hand.

Door hanging

The doors are hung using 2in brass butts.

Glazing

3mm glass is used with silicon sealant to hold the glass in place. Once the sealant has set, putty the glass in.

Shelves

The shelves are 6mm toughened glass. The holes for shelf studs are drilled with a template.

Handles

Make the drawer handles by drilling out 40mm discs on the drill press with a proprietary hole saw. This should contain a 6mm pilot drill, so leave this in. Make enough 'petals' using a 20mm plug cutter.

Working from the drawing, mark off the corners of the petals and shape them to fit, using a disc sander. Glue and cramp the petals onto the discs. Finger clearance is created with a

wooden washer. To make this, clamp a thick piece of MDF onto the drill press bed, then drill down with the 6mm bit. Drill some 6mm holes through a section of timber of the required clearance. Take out the 6mm drill bit, replacing it with the 20mm plug cutter. Place a tight 6mm dowel piece into the hole in the bed. By placing the now drilled timber onto the dowel, the wooden washers can be made. Clean off and then glue-up the handle front, washer and dowel.

For the door handles, the 6mm drill bit must be removed to make the 40mm discs. Cut and disc-sand them down to create two matching halves, then screw and glue them to the piece which will be dovetailed into the doors. Glue on three petals, then disc-sand them down.

Finish

Apply three coats of Danish oil over a period of one week, and then lightly de-nib and wax the surface. ■

Harold Wilson, of Sutton Coldfield in the West Midlands, is a self-taught woodworker and has won two awards in the F&C Furniture Competition at the ATME.

PHOTOGRAPHY BY ANTHONY BAILEY
ILLUSTRATIONS BY SIMON RODWAY

Harold Wilson

makes a mahogany
side cabinet

**A dainty way to
downsize from a sideboard**

Through a side cabinet, darkly

This cabinet was constructed for a friend who required a smaller cabinet to replace a standard sideboard. The brief was the cabinet should be 'dainty and of a dark mahogany colour'. In addition, I considered it essential the top should be resistant to warm dishes and liquid spills.

The overall dimensions of the cabinet would be: 760mm wide by 850mm high by 410mm deep (30 by 33⅜ by 16¾6in).

Timber preparation

The seasoned timber was machined to oversized pieces and stored in the workshop for four weeks to condition. It was then accurately machined to actual sizes on a Felder universal machine. I find this process of conditioning and final finishing gives good results, since no matter how well seasoned a piece of wood may be, changes in temperature – and particularly humidity – tend to make the material change shape.

Construction

The side frames of the carcass are constructed using traditional mortice and tenon joints; the tenons being 12.5mm (½in) thick. Also, the lower front and back rails are morticed into the side frames. A frame is constructed using mortice and tenons for the lower drawer runners; this frame is jointed into the side frames using twin-stub tenons. Similarly, the upper frame is constructed to an identical size, but jointing into the

Moulding on drawer front

Top moulding detail

*'The seasoned timber
was machined to
oversized pieces and
stored in the workshop
for four weeks to
condition'*

Drawers stop and kicker

top of the side frames is achieved using dovetails. This arrangement is necessary in order to enable the upright rail between the two drawers to be fitted. It should be noted here the runners protrude by 12mm (½in) at each end of the frames to allow the guides to be attached later. The upright rail between the two drawers is twin-stub tenoned into the horizontal rails.

Grooves are cut on the inside of the side frame members to take the panels. The grooves are 6 by 6mm (¼ by ¼in) and cut with a slot cutter using a router table. Care must be exercised in this operation so the grooves stop at the mortice holes. I always chamfer the outside of the bottom rails at 30° in order to reduce the possibility of dust being trapped when the finished cabinet is in use.

The side panels are cut to size from sapele-veneered 6mm (¼in) ply, making sure there is slight movement in the grooves to allow for dimensional changes. This results from the humidity

and temperature changes of the cabinet in use. At this stage, too, the legs are shaped on both inside edges. The shapes were cut initially on a bandsaw and finished on a drum sander. This shaping enhances the cabinet by making it appear lighter and more delicate, while not reducing its strength significantly. Here, 6mm (¼in) deep rebates are also cut in the rear rails to take the 6mm (¼in) ply back.

Assembly

Before gluing up the side frames with PVA adhesive, the inside edges of the frames and both sides of the panels are finished with two coats of clear shellac. After each coat hardens, the surface is carefully cut back with 240-grit paper. Final finishing is achieved with Fiddes rich mahogany wax polish which is

applied liberally with 0000 steel wool. Final buffing with a soft clean cloth achieved the desired result.

The assembly of the side frames involves careful application of the adhesive to the mortice holes. Obviously, sufficient glue must be applied to produce a good joint, but excessive amounts of glue result in a lengthy clean-up operation. Another factor that many people find difficult is the positioning and holding of the sash cramps and protective blocks of wood. This problem can be overcome, I have found, by attaching softwood blocks to the cramp head surfaces with double-sided tape.

The side frames are cleaned-up to a fine finish, since it's much easier to obtain the desired result at this stage than when the cabinet is complete.

Adjustable shelf detail

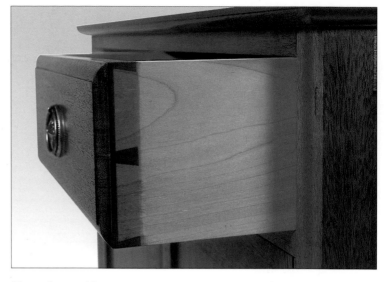

Cherry drawer sides

'When using adhesives the concept of working time is important. It can be defined as the time available for mixing and manipulating the material before any significant setting occurs'

Glue up

The next gluing-up stage involves the lower rails and lower drawer runner frame. Obviously, this is more time-consuming, hence the sash cramps must be carefully set to the correct dimensions. Needless to say, the softwood blocks attached to cramp heads are a tremendous help at this stage. Also, in order to allow sufficient time for the gluing and cramping, a slower-setting adhesive is helpful. In this case I use Cascamite which has a considerably longer working time than the PVA adhesives.

When using adhesives the concept of working time is important. It can be defined as the time available for mixing and manipulating the material before any significant setting occurs. Similarly, the time for the adhesive to set to a state where cramps can be removed can be termed the 'setting time'. Both working times and setting times are dependent upon external factors, particularly temperature. I think it would be helpful if manufacturers gave an indication of these times on the containers for a range of temperatures.

The upper frame and short vertical rail can now be glued up using sash cramps. Making the two frames parallel is achieved using spacers between the frames.

Drawers

The drawer fronts are machined from a board of ripple mahogany (*Khaya* spp) to 25mm (1in) thick. The sides and back are 10mm (⅜in) thick cherry (*Prunus* spp). Lap-dovetails are used at the front and through-dovetails at the back. Grooves 5 by 5mm (³⁄₁₆ by ³⁄₁₆in) are cut in the inner surfaces of the sides and front at a distance of 10mm (⅜in) from the lower edge. The spacing of the dovetails is planed so the grooves do not break through the sides of the drawer. The lower edge of the drawer back is 15mm (⁹⁄₁₆in) above the lower edge of the sides.

Drawer bottoms are cut from 4mm (⁵⁄₃₂in) ply and green baize is attached to the inner surface with rubber-based impact adhesive. When attaching fabrics to board it is important to apply the adhesive uniformly to the board surface and allow it to almost dry before applying the fabric. If the fabric is applied too early the adhesive will penetrate the fabric producing unsightly marks.

The drawers are assembled using a minimal amount of adhesive; the joints gently tapped home with a hammer and block, and then checked for squareness and flatness. The following day the drawers are cleaned up and fitted into their openings. Guides are attached to the runners using screws and final adjustments made so each drawer will slide smoothly without any sloppiness. A moulding is cut on the outside edges of the drawers.

Doors

It is necessary to ensure the widths together of the two doors is 6mm (¼in) more than the opening – this allows for the rebates at the opening edges. Mortices 8mm (⁵⁄₁₆in) wide are cut in the stiles and the corresponding tenons in the cross rails. The door panels are prepared oversize from 6mm (¼in) ply. These are then veneered with selected mahogany using a vacuum press and this results in flat matching panels. Grooves 6mm (¼in) deep are cut in the inner edges of the door frames wide enough to take the panels.

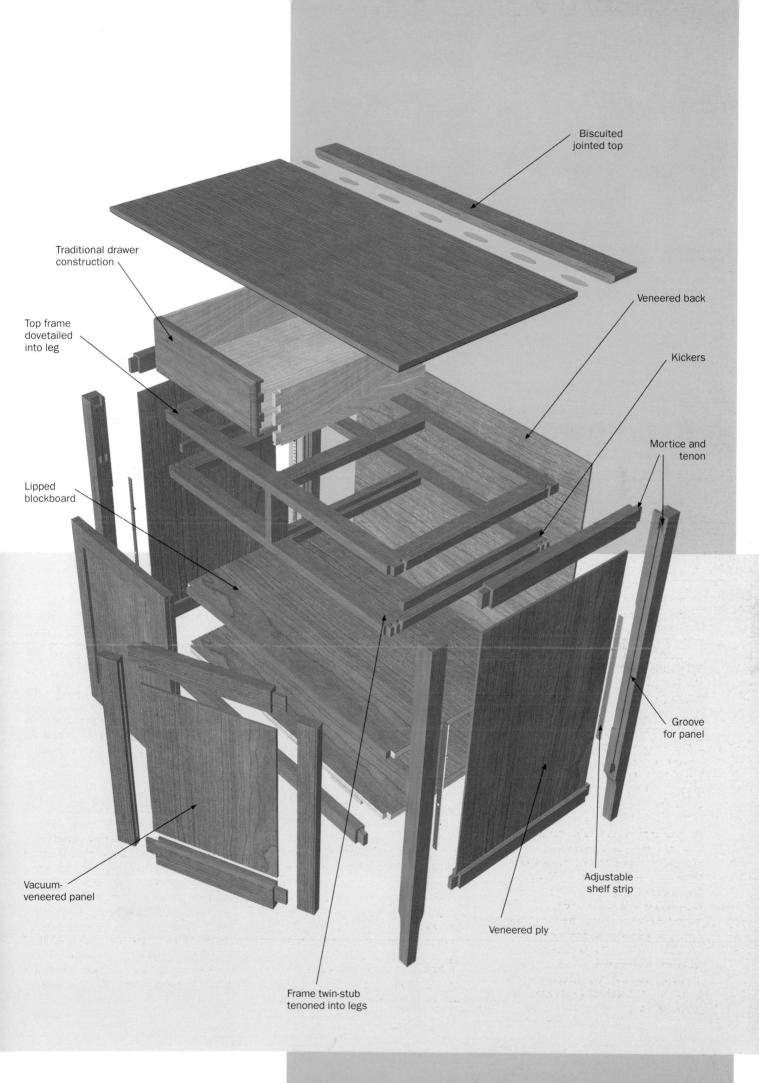

Biscuited
jointed top

Traditional drawer
construction

Top frame
dovetailed
into leg

Veneered back

Kickers

Mortice and
tenon

Lipped
blockboard

Groove
for panel

Vacuum-
veneered panel

Frame twin-stub
tenoned into legs

Veneered ply

Adjustable
shelf strip

Finishing

Prior to finishing, all the fittings are removed, together with the shelves, top and back. The shelves and back are finished with three coats of Rustin's acrylic varnish, rubbing each coat down with 240-grit silicon carbide paper before applying the next coat. The advantage of this finish is it leaves very little odour – a real advantage for inside cabinets. The remainder of the cabinet, with the exception of the top, is finished with two coats of clear shellac and Fiddes wax polish, in order to blend with the previously finished panels. The top is finished with six coats of Rustin's Plastic Coating applied at one-hour intervals on the same day. After hardening for a few days, the top is carefully 'matted down' with 280-grit wet/dry paper used wet. This produces a flat matt surface; then burnished, with the paste provided, to the desired degree of sheen. This finish is extremely serviceable, it's resistant to heat and solvents, and is therefore ideal for cabinet and table tops. Also, it has great clarity so the grain structure is not hidden. The disadvantage of Plastic Coating is its name! I hope the manufacturers will find a more suitable name to describe its superior properties – such as 'heat resistant lacquer'! Another disadvantage of this product is its intense odour in use, which necessitates thorough ventilation. In spite of this it's still my choice of material for cabinet tops. I finished a dining table with this product 25 years ago and the clarity and surface are still extremely good.

'The cabinet is completed by fitting a ring handle to each drawer and a matching escutcheon over the keyhole'

Bottom support detail

Rebate on door stop style

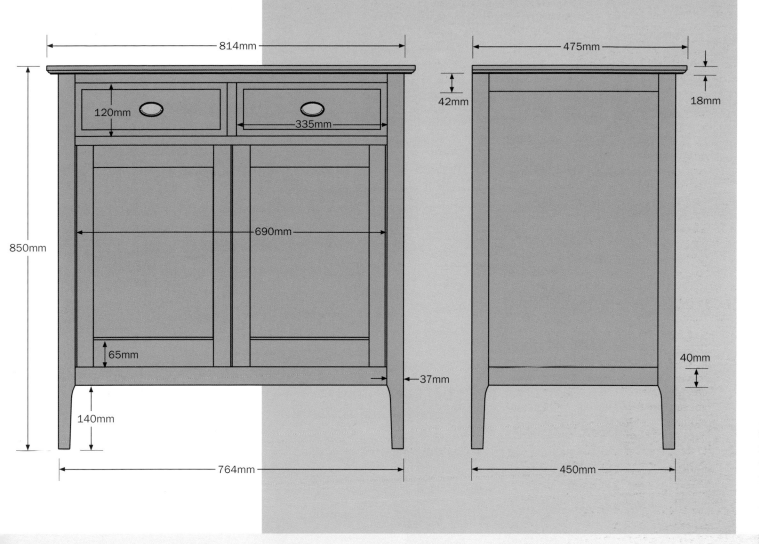

The panels are fitted into the frames allowing for slight movement in use. As in the case of the side frames, both panels and inner edges of the frames are finished before assembly. After assembly, the doors are cleaned up and fitted to the opening. Housings for the hinges are cut and the hinge sunk to its full thickness in the door. I prefer this method to sinking the hinge half in the door and half in the cabinet frame for two reasons. Firstly, from an aesthetic viewpoint, it does not break the line of the hinge edge of the door, particularly when a matching bead is worked along the door edge as in this case. Secondly, any discrepancy in cutting the depth of the hinge housing could be doubled if the hinge is sunk in both door and cabinet rails.

The opening edges of the doors are rebated: the rebate in the left door at the front, whilst the rebate for the right-hand door is at the back. Also, a bead is worked in the front edge of the right hand door to match the beads at the outer edges. Flat bolts are fitted at the top and bottom of the left-hand door and a lock fitted to the right-hand door.

Top and shelves

Since wide boards are not available, the top is prepared from several pieces of 60 by 18mm (2⅜ by ⅞in) mahogany biscuit jointed together. This method produced a stable board and the joints are barely perceptible after planing. The top is squared to size and an ovolo moulding is cut in the underside of the front and side edges. The top is fitted to the cabinet using conventional hardwood buttons to allow movement due to changing ambient conditions.

Two adjustable shelves are cut from 18mm (2³⁄₃₂in) thick mahogany-faced blockboard. Both long edges are lipped with mahogany using biscuits and the front edges moulded with a double bead. This produces a kind edge to the touch and makes the shelf appear slimmer.

The fittings for the adjustable shelves consist of raised bookcase strip which is cut to length and screwed to the inside edges of the uprights. Matching raised bookcase studs can then be placed in suitable positions for the required spacing of the shelves.

Fittings and handles

The cabinet is completed by fitting a ring handle to each drawer and a matching escutcheon over the keyhole. The manufacturers assume the handles will be fitted by passing the threaded stud at the back of the handle through a hole in the drawer front and securing with a nut inside the drawer.

This method is unsightly and harsh to the touch. I prefer to use a stopped hole in the drawer front and cut the studding to match. The handle is then fixed using epoxy resin adhesive thus retaining the flush surface inside the drawer. The fittings come in an 'antique finish' which clashed with the brass hinges, so in order to overcome this problem the hinges are treated with Liberon Tourmaline Brown – cold patinating fluid – which produces a similar finish on the hinges to that on the other fittings.

The construction is completed by fitting a 6mm (¼in) plywood back into rebates in the cabinet using 18mm (2³⁄₃₂in) screws. ■

Compact storage

Derek Smith makes a CD rack

T HE STORAGE of cassettes and compact discs poses a dilemma. Do you store them on display or in a cabinet? If on display, they can be seen vertically or horizontally, if in a cabinet, they can be put into drawers and viewed from above.

● **DEREK SMITH began his woodworking career with a traditional apprenticeship and then worked for the London firm, Waring and Gillows. He started his own business, Fine Wood Furniture, in 1971 and continues to make one-off pieces to commission**

RIGHT: The north American oak of the main carcass is relieved with the fine detail of the inlaid black walnut squares

'...as soon as the details were finalized there was a cloud of dust as I left the office and headed for the workshop – I know where I would rather be!'

Most of the storage systems I make for clients tend to be variations of the latter, but I wanted to make one for myself, and I like the look of compact discs – not strewn around the floor, you understand, but neatly stored and accessible. The shape of this holder lends itself to both horizontal and vertical racking, with the advantages and disadvantages of both. When they are horizontally stacked you don't have to twist your neck to read the spines, but then the quantity of CDs stored is reduced to about half because they need to slide in and out on supports. I decided that a little twist of the neck was a small price to pay for double the capacity.

Preparation

I spent a lot of time working on different ideas and considerations, but as soon as the details were finalized there was a cloud of dust as I left the office and headed for the workshop – I know where I would rather be!

American white oak (*Quercus alba princus*) was used with inlay squares of American black walnut (*Juglans nigra*). When all the measurements were decided, I made a mock-up using pine sides and plywood shelves – I do this with most projects – ok, it takes a little extra time but it can save you hours of work, whether you are a professional or an amateur.

Prepare a cutting list – I tend to make full drawings for smaller items with the grain direction marked to avoid ending up with, in this case, five small shelves that are not quite square, with the grain going in the wrong direction.

Prepare all the components to size.

Shelves

The shelves are the first pieces to work, and can either be biscuit-jointed or dowelled. Using biscuits is so easy, but for many years I dowelled, and as long as you spend some time making decent, accurate jigs they are successful – with the added advantage that, unlike biscuits, the joint will not slip as you glue up, which sometimes happens with flat dowels like splines and tongues.

When you have dowelled or biscuited the shelves transfer the centre lines to the side and complete the corresponding holes/slots.

'...I tend to make full drawings for smaller items with the grain direction marked to avoid ending up with, in this case, five small shelves that are not quite square, with the grain going in the wrong direction

'I like the idea of flared sides with tall narrow pieces – visually it makes them appear firmly anchored to the floor'

Sides

The sides are 18mm ($^{11}/_{16}$in) at the top, flaring out to 25mm (1in) at the base. I like the idea of flared sides with tall narrow pieces – visually it makes them appear firmly anchored to the floor. Shape the flare of the sides on the bandsaw or the surfacer, removing most of the waste, and finish by hand with a sharp plane. If you do not possess a bandsaw, plane them by hand, working with the grain – save this job for a cold morning as it will soon warm you up!

BELOW: **CD rack empty showing interior shelf spaces**

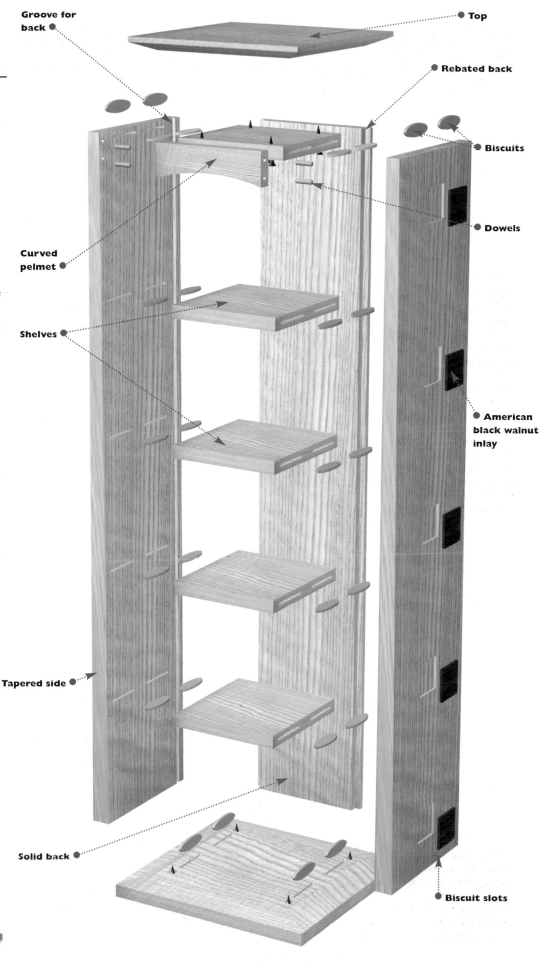

Groove for back

Top

Rebated back

Biscuits

Curved pelmet

Dowels

Shelves

American black walnut inlay

Tapered side

Solid back

Biscuit slots

> '**The base is prepared from a solid section because it will match the direction of the grain of the top and it saves mitering the corners**'

Next, cut the groove that the back lets into, using a router or spindle moulder – it is 6mm (¼in) wide, 6mm (¼in) deep and 10mm (⅜in) from the back edge.

The last thing to do on the sides is to dowel/biscuit at the top and the bottom.

Base

The base is prepared from a solid section because it will match the direction of the grain of the top and it saves mitering the corners. Cut the angle oversize on the table saw, leaving plenty to plane up by hand in case it starts to burn, or the saw blade digs in. If you don't have a table saw, work the angles by hand with a sharp smoothing plane.

Next, biscuit/dowel the base to correspond with the sides.

Top

The top has a 115mm (4½in) diameter hole cut in the centre so that a plant container can stand in it, but that is of course optional. Prepare the top as you did the base, using a solid piece and cutting the hole before you plane the angles. The best way to form the hole is to use a router with a jig, again remembering to allow extra for the guide bush. Alternatively, cut it with

a coping saw and finish off the inside with a bobbin sander, sanding drum on a drill press, or by hand. Start with coarser grits finishing with fine.

Pelmet

The pelmet can be straight or curved and is secured into the sides with small dowels. Cut the curve on the bandsaw, or with a coping saw, after you have dowelled – it is easier to hold a square piece of wood in the vice when dowelling.

Back

A solid piece of timber was used so that the CD holder could be positioned anywhere in a room and look as good from the back as from the front.

The back lets into the sides, in the grooves that you have already machined, but does not let into the top or base, so it needs to be cross-cut accurately.

Machine the back and then rebate the sides along the grain so that they fit into the groove with 1mm (¹⁄₁₆in) clearance at the sides in case of any expansion (*see diagram*).

Finishing

Sand all components, starting with coarser grits and working down to fine.

On most of my work I try to finish all surfaces before I glue-up. I know this is not always possible but as I use mainly solid timber, and the temperature in my workshop is never going to be the same as my clients' centrally heated houses, a door panel contracting even 0.5mm (0.01in) can leave a very annoying line against the door style.

Finish all the interior surfaces, as this is going to be difficult once everything is glued, and it is far easier to wipe the glue off a sealed surface.

At this stage also finish the top, base and back, on both sides. Don't worry about the exterior of the sides and the front at this stage.

I have access to spraying facilities and most of the items I produce are finished with either acid catalyst lacquer or two-pack polyurethane, mainly because, in domestic interiors, they tend to have to put up with everyday use and sometimes, dare I say it, abuse.

If you cannot spray finish, use a semi-matt polyurethane finish with a good quality brush, thinning the first coats and rubbing down in between with fine paper or wire wool.

Gluing up

With everything at the ready –

> '**A solid piece of timber was used so that the CD holder could be positioned anywhere in a room and look as good from the back as from the front**'

INLAID SQUARES

The inlay squares are a matter of personal choice to the maker, but I felt that the sides needed some relief. If you decide to inlay, plane up a piece of contrasting wood 40mm (1½in) wide and 4mm (⅛in) thick – I used American black walnut.

If you have a router, it is best to make a jig. Use a piece of ply wider than the side and then screw two pieces of wood each side of the ply so that it can slide the length of the solid side, with no play. When you cut the square in the ply remember to allow extra for the guide bush – this will depend on the size cutter you use.

Plunge the holes to 3mm (⅛in) deep, finish off the corners with a sharp chisel, and after cross-cutting the solid inlay piece to length, glue them in.

Leave to dry, and then plane level by hand with a sharp plane.

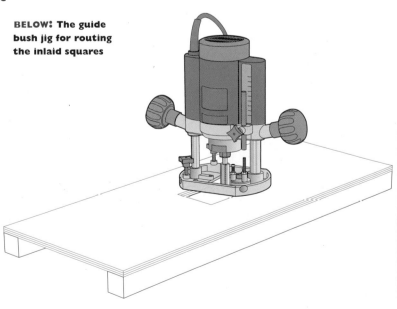

BELOW: The guide bush jig for routing the inlaid squares

cramps, softwood blocks, damp cloth and flat biscuits or dowels – start by gluing dowels in the ends of the shelves. Work as fast as you can and then glue the shelves into one side.

Wipe off any excess glue as you go and then tap home the other side with a rubber mallet or hammer and block. Stand the unit upright and then cramp the shelves home using masking tape to hold the softwood blocks, and check for square.

When the glue has hardened, check that the shelves are flush with the front and back. If there are any discrepancies, adjust them with a smoothing plane and sand.

Check the sides to make sure there are no marks from the cramping block, then glue and biscuit the base on – I also secure this with four brass screws. Slide the back in and then biscuit and glue the top into position.

Now finish sealing the front, back edges and the sides. ∎

BELOW: The back is rebated and grooved into the sides of the carcass

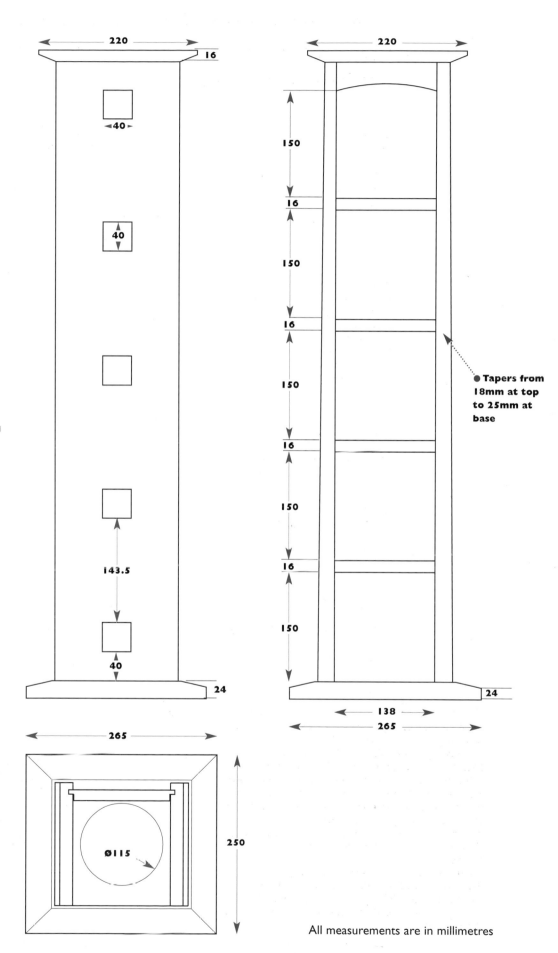

Tapers from 18mm at top to 25mm at base

All measurements are in millimetres

Mark Ripley gained a BA (Hons) degree in 3D Design at Leicester Polytechnic where he specialised in furniture design and making. For the next 10 years Mark divided his time between teaching woodwork to handicapped adults and furniture-making; for the past seven years has devoted all his time to designing and making furniture. He has a workshop in a converted farm building at South Moreton, Oxfordshire

PHOTOGRAPHY BY MANI CEFAI
ILLUSTRATIONS BY SIMON RODWAY

Contemporary feel in design and timber but traditional in construction

Chest beater

Mark Ripley makes a chest of drawers for a master bedroom

This chest of drawers – and two complementary bedside cabinets – were designed for the master bedroom of a spacious apartment. The clients knew what they wanted the pieces to do, but were open-minded about the design. One proviso was the pieces should be 'clearly a one-off, without being wacky'. My work is quite traditional, so there was little chance of this piece being too over-the-top.

Design and timber

The design was composed of traditional elements with a slightly unusual configuration, aimed at creating a balanced asymmetry while retaining practicality. Fortunately, my first proposal was accepted and we quickly proceeded to viewing samples of proposed materials.

I would never suggest a wood like olive ash (*Fraxinus* spp) unless I had already found a supply. In fact, Alec Golesworthy at Timberpride had been trying to sell me some for a while and it's nice stuff. Nonetheless, a lot of wastage must be accounted for in order to ensure consistent colour. Alec also supplied the white ash (*Fraxinus americana*) and the English oak (*Quercus robur*) for the drawer linings. I usually use American white ash for its consistent colour but was assured this really was white, and ordered several cubic feet on the basis of a small offcut. The oak was bought as 19mm (¾in) but was actually slightly under. However, it

was so flat and clean it machined up beautifully, and despite some worrying moments with stick marks I was very happy with the prepared cutting list.

The selection of components from rough-sawn stock through to planing and dimensioning can be a nerve-racking process as well as a physically tiring one, but once accomplished I could settle down and enjoy making the piece.

Customers visiting my workshop for the first time are often surprised to see their furniture starts out as large slices of tree, often with the bark still on! I like them to visit at least once if possible to get an idea of the work that goes into a one-off commission. The timber for all three of this client's pieces was

Drawers

The drawer fronts are prepared from three boards 250mm (9¾in) wide and 1500mm (59in) long finished at 22mm (⅞in). The selection of the drawer fronts is particularly important here because of the contrasting colour. Having the grain running through from one side of the piece to the other ties the whole thing together visually. The linings – drawer sides and backs – are finished at 11mm (⁷⁄₁₆in). Given the size of the bigger drawers this is too narrow to fit the bottoms into grooves so drawer slips are used.

Veneered ply is used for the bottoms. This is strong, stable and economical and I generally use veneered ply for drawer bottoms in preference to solid wood. Olive ash is used for the slips to create visual interest inside the drawer.

The individual drawer components are fitted into the main carcass before the joints are marked out. The fronts are cut marginally oversize and then very slightly bevelled all round by hand until they push into their opening by about half their thickness. Recesses are routed into the underside of the drawer fronts to correspond with the recesses on the cabinet frame. A simple template is made for this, which is screwed to a batten enabling the template to be clamped to the drawer front.

As with the fronts, the sides are cut about 1mm (³⁄₆₄in) overwidth and then slightly tapered until they enter by about half their length. If possible, the grain should run from front to back of the drawer so when cleaning up and fitting later you are planing away from the front, and not towards it. The backs are scribed off the fronts for length.

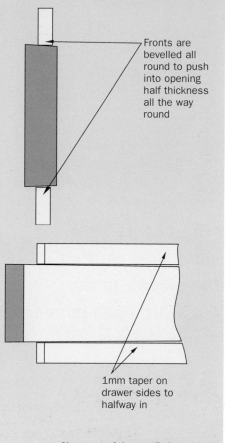

Fronts are bevelled all round to push into opening half thickness all the way round

1mm taper on drawer sides to halfway in

Nuances of drawer fitting

Routing the finger slots in the drawer front bottom

The template for the slots

The completed finger slot and scallop

Inside the carcass, showing the drawer runner strips

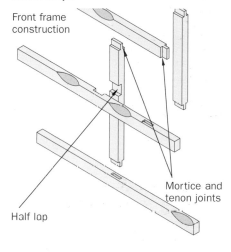

Front frame construction

Half lap

Mortice and tenon joints

prepared at the same time, though the stock for the small cabinets and drawers for the chest was put into stick for later use.

Construction

The jointed up boards for the top and ends are prepared, and then faced off with a bench plane. This was a pure delight and boded well for workablity in the joint making. This stage is, I reckon, to be about a third of the way through a project and is a good time to work on finishes, jigs and fittings if these have not been finalised already.

The construction consists of a frame and veneered plywood panel back screwed to the solid wood ends. The front frame is biscuit jointed to the end panels. The plinth is a separate carcass and the top is screwed to the main cabinet after assembly. Because the drawer runners are so complex they are fitted after the assembly of the cabinet. To incorporate them in the main construction would have resulted in an impossible glue up.

Front frame is biscuited on to the main carcass

Plinth support blocks

Plinth with bevelled lipping located on rebated fillet

'The clients knew what they wanted the pieces to do, but were open-minded about the design'

Mortice and tenons are used for all but one of the front frame joints, the exception being a single cross-halving. Apart from the corners, the tenons are all the width of the rails. This saves time and because the inner faces of the frame will eventually be covered by the drawers any marginal discrepancy will not show. It goes without saying that marking out the joints for the front frame is critical.

At this point the recesses for the handles are cut. I had visions of a clever routing jig to do this but a mock-up of the handle detail made on the bandsaw revealed a jig would be difficult to make, so the bandsaw was an efficient alternative. The curve is marked on the frame and the bandsaw table set to 45°. With a careful touch and a sharp 6mm (¼in) blade, the cut is quite straightforward. The job is finished on the end of the linisher.

A full dry assembly is required before gluing up, to check for fits and overall accuracy. It's necessary to glue and clamp the frame in a number of operations.

Back frame

This is a reasonably straightforward procedure. Remember, the back frame is shorter than the front frame by the combined thickness of the end panels. For simplicity the three vertical components are all tenoned and the mortices are in the corresponding top and bottom rails. Dry-assemble and face off the frame before dismantling to rout the grooves for the back panels. It's important to check the router cutter against the thickness of the ply. A 6mm (¼in) router cutter will be just that, but 6mm ply may be anything from 5 to 7mm (³⁄₁₆ to ⁹⁄₃₂in). Fortunately for me this time it all matched, but it doesn't always!

The end panels, back frame and front frame now need to be justified so they are exactly the same height and the correct widths. Once trued up the battens can be fitted, which will take the drawer runners. These are 10mm (³⁄₈in) square except where additional depth is required to enter the recess formed by the back panels. They're screwed in place – on the ply back ▶

Dovetails

A marking gauge is used to mark the length and width of the dovetails. These are marginally less than the thickness of the linings – except on the ends of the drawer fronts – to allow for planing in after assembly. The setting out of the dovetails on the front is largely an aesthetic decision but where the drawer sizes vary, the dovetails gradually get bigger towards the bottom of the piece while the pins remain the same size.

Grooves are cut in the fronts to take the bottoms. These run straight through and will be covered by the lap dovetails. The drawer backs are cut to their finished height which will allow the bottom to run underneath.

Dovetails can be cut effectively with a bandsaw and the waste cleaned out with coping saw and chisel down to the scribed mark made by the gauge. The pins are scribed off the dovetails with a marking knife and are cut with a dovetail saw. Much of the waste between the pins can be removed with a router which produces a perfectly flat face, the remaining corners being cleaned up with a chisel. The joints are masked off and the insides of the drawers are waxed prior to assembly. I pull the joints in with sash cramps as this is gentler than the traditional hammer and seems to make a tighter joint. Finally, the drawers are cleaned up and fitted with a constantly sharpened bench plane before sanding and waxing. The runners are also waxed to ease running.

The slips are prepared, glued and clamped in place and the drawer bottoms fitted. The bottom can distort a drawer so care is required; it can work for you though if a drawer is slightly out!

I'm aware the method outlined above differs in some respects from traditional practice and other makers will have developed their own variations, but such developments keep both our craft and its traditions alive.

Traditionally lapped dovetails on fronts

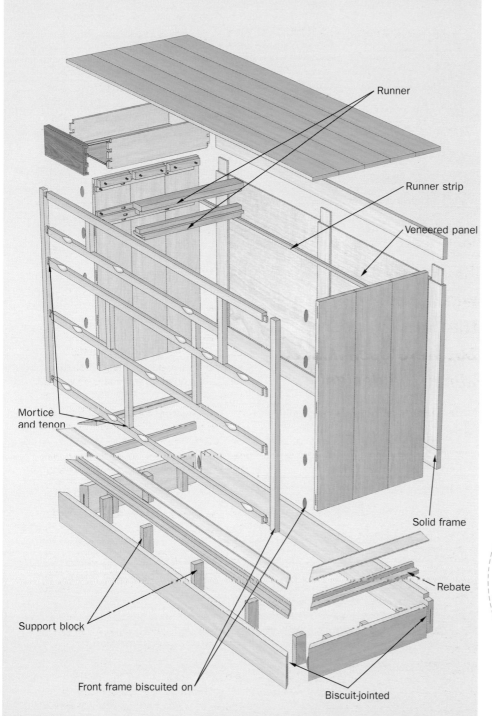

Runner

Runner strip

Veneered panel

Mortice
and tenon

Solid frame

Rebate

Support block

Front frame biscuited on

Biscuit-jointed

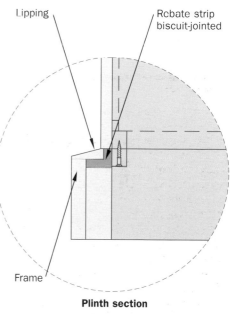

Lipping

Rebate strip
biscuit-jointed

Frame

Plinth section

> panels screwed from the back – from inside the cabinet.

Assembly begins with the end panels and back, which are glued, screwed and plugged. The front frame is biscuit-jointed to the end panels.

Plinth

This is a complicated construction when made from 25mm (1in) ex-stock. From 50mm (2in) material it would be quick and simple, but may run the risk of the mitres opening up over the wider joint. So, for 22mm (⅞in) finished stock, the process is as follows . . .

A simple carcass is constructed using biscuits for butt joints at the back, and mitres at the front. The back piece of the plinth is 15mm (⅝in) higher than the rest to allow for the addition of the bevelled lipping. Rebated strips are biscuit jointed around the inside top of the front and ends of the plinth, and trued up to provide an even face for the lipping. Reinforcing blocks are glued into the corners of the plinth and at intervals to the front and ends. These strengthen the joints and create a load bearing structure. The outside corners of the mitres are routed and lipped to give

protection to this exposed area. A bandsaw is used to cut the bevels for the lippings which are cut oversize and planed back after being glued in place. The deep chamfers on the top are hand-planed, allowing a margin for final fitting.

Setting up

Fixing the plinth and top to the main carcass is done with small screwed blocks. At the top and bottom of the end panels these double as drawer runners. At the front and back, screw blocks are used again. At the front these

Runners and kickers

Central runners and kickers

> ## 'The drawer fronts – in order to maximise the colour contrast – are finished with Danish oil'

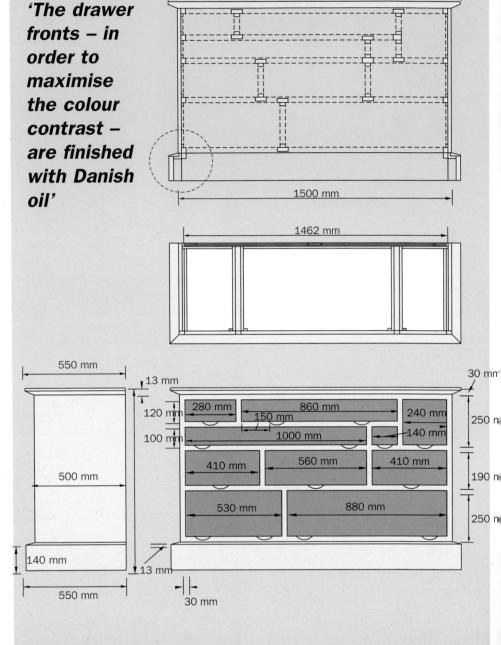

Drawer runner and kicker arrangement

need to be rebated to fit onto the plinth. I spent a whole day on this job, setting up, planing in the top and bottom chamfers, checking for square and fine sanding! It's an effort that certainly pays off when it comes to fitting the drawers. The whole job can now be sealed and to retain the lightness of the ash I used a clear water-based lacquer.

Drawer runners

As indicated earlier, the solution to this problem is driven by pragmatism rather than elegance. The runners at the ends of the cabinet are slot-screwed. These

are planed to the width of the frame members. Additional strips are prepared to fit above and below these to guide the sides of the drawers. Again, these are slot-screwed to allow for movement in the solid carcass sides.

The internal runners are cut to length and notched to fit onto the battens fitted earlier. These are screwed in place using 50 by 19mm (2 by ¾in) No. 6 screws at each end. Battens planed to the width of the front frame are screwed to the runners to guide the drawer sides. This is a full day's work and then some!

Supporting the cabinet on its end gave

the best access, but final checking must be done when the piece is set up level and true on its base.

Finishing

The lacquer is cut back and two further coats applied; then cutback with 320g silicon carbide paper and given three coats of clear finishing wax before finally burnishing with 0000 wire wool. The drawer fronts – in order to maximise the colour contrast – are finished with Danish oil. ∎

John Bullar first caught the attention of Furniture and Cabinetmaking magazine readers when he entered a competition to produce a twisted dovetail. He entered a box section with four different versions and won a pair of Japanese chisels! John has a degree in engineering, which influences his approach to woodwork

PHOTOGRAPHY BY JOHN BULLAR
ILLUSTRATIONS BY IAN HALL (MAIN)
AND SIMON RODWAY

John Bullar makes an Arts & Crafts style cabinet

Following the traditions of craftsmen like Sidney Barnsley

In their footsteps

Travelling home from the Axminster/*F&C* show a few years ago, I stopped off near Cheltenham to stay with some old friends. We took a trip into town and spent some happy hours in the Cheltenham Museum. This has a gallery devoted to the Cotswold school of Arts & Crafts furniture – inspiring pieces of work from mid-19th to mid-20th century with a common theme of 'pleasure in unpretentious handcraft'.

I came away wanting to design and build some furniture that would express a few of the ideas I had seen. Immediately, I started sketching while my memory was fresh . . . I would start by making a sideboard cabinet and follow it with a coordinated round table, both pieces for a large kitchen.

One fundamental of the Cotswold style was to use wide boards to give uninterrupted figuring on surfaces. I wanted the sideboard top to be made from a single board without any joints, but I would have to find the right wood.

Timber: elm

Some of the finest furniture in the gallery, even quite large pieces, was in English walnut (*Juglans* spp) which is certainly beautiful to work and to behold, but large pieces are in short supply. I have only ever been able to obtain enough good-quality material to use it for small, delicate work and haven't come across English walnut boards wide enough for this work.

Instead, I decided to use elm (*Ulmus procera*), a beautifully wild, organic-figured wood with bags of character. It has warm brown colours with occasional streaks of green and a profusion of cat's-paw knots. The downside of elm's wild nature is that it can move a lot while drying. It can twist and buckle around the knots and nearly always splits around the central pith of the tree as it weaves up through the trunk. A hundred years ago elm was mainly used for coffins and probably never dried. For furniture-making it must be dried thoroughly then kept that way, which is quite possible now, with central heating.

So, when I got the chance of flat-sawn boards, all more than 660mm (26in) wide by 25mm (1in) and 2mm (⅛in) thick, carefully air-dried, and with good figuring, I snapped up six consecutive planks – enough to make the surfaces of a sideboard and table. At the same time I bought about 16ft of 200mm by 75mm (8in by 3in) from the same tree.

Handles

The handles are made from brown oak in the style of some traditional Cotswold Arts & Crafts pieces, with upper and lower tactile concave surfaces for a finger and thumb grip.

Turn the brown oak first to produce a matching pair of 'wheels' rather like heavy-duty castors about 75mm (3in) diameter. From each wheel, bandsaw out a central strip and discard it, leaving two sector-shaped handles.

Book-matched drawer fronts

The drawers are made in the conventional hand-dovetailed manner with elm fronts, quarter-sawn oak sides and cedar of Lebanon (Cedrus libani) bases. As with the rest of the cabinet front, the drawer fronts are book-matched by choosing a pair of consecutive boards.

The sides are joined to the front with stopped dovetails and to the rear with through dovetails. The cedar bases are slotted into the sides and rear.

Doors

The doors are of frame and panel construction. The stiles and rails are jointed using open-slotted mortices and full-size tenons. The vertical and horizontal cross-members meet in a halving joint and have small tenons to engage in the same slots as the panels. All the door parts are cut from adjacent boards to keep them looking 'book-matched', the rails and stiles are straight-grained and the panels from burred ends of boards.

After cutting all the joints the rails and stiles are slotted to take the panels and cross-members. I hand-planed the chamfers on all the panels using a No. 78 rebate plane with a spur cutter which I keep sharp to give a clean profile.

Then assemble the door in the normal manner.

Dovetails

With so many dovetail joints on the carcass corners, I find it's difficult to force them together if they are tight, yet the slightest gaps would be very conspicuous.

For normal dovetails, on drawer sides and the like, I usually knife-mark the top of the pins from the underside of the tails. Sadly, there's no way I could cut the required accuracy through inch-thick dovetails using this technique. Instead I had to work out a method so the visible surfaces would be marked directly off one another.

Selection

I selected the boards very carefully when I bought them. They had already been air-dried. I had them kilned, then collected them within a day of coming out of the kiln. After several months' storage in my workshop, most of the boards remained completely flat while the ends had cupped by a few millimetres. I picked through the boards for the cabinet top and sides to give an appearance of continuous figuring 'wrapped' around the top corner joints. I wanted the finished carcass to be a full 25mm (1in) thick.

Stepped pedestal feet

The carcass of this cabinet sits upon a pair of fairly massive pedestals. They are joined by a back and front stretcher rail dovetailed into each pedestal. The pedestals are undercut to form front and rear feet, and with stepped fronts. These are cut from 75 by 152mm (3 by 6in) clm, so the front end-grain patterns are book-matched. The cutaways are made on the bandsaw, together with a morticing chisel to remove the angled undercut of the feet.

Use a finely tuned block plane to form chamfers where possible; where the block plane would not reach, I used a long-handled Japanese paring chisel to complete the finely cut chamfers.

DOOR FRAMES

The door frame joints are cut on the bandsaw with shims to space the pieces accurately off the fence. Only two shims are needed to make two cuts for the tenon sides and two cuts for the mortice sides. One shim is the exact thickness of the bandsaw blade kerf, the other the exact width of the tenon. The bandsaw must be accurately set up with the blade at right angles to the table in both directions and the fence exactly parallel to the blade. The cuts should be made using the outer surface of the stiles and rails as a reference face against the fence as follows: adjust the fence to make the deepest cuts on each end of the stiles. These will form the inner surfaces of the tenons. The fence stays in position for the following cuts.

Cut the outer faces of the tenons, using both the blade-width shim and the tenon-width shim together between the stile and the fence. Cut each end of each rail to form the matching face of the mortice using only the blade width shim. The other sides of the mortices are cut on the rails using the tenon-width shim alone. The tenon shoulders can then be cut on the bandsaw using a sliding fence. The mortices are removed from their slots with a pillar drill, then cleaned up with a chisel.

This is a swift and precise method of making strong joints but it is certainly worth having a dummy run on scrap to make sure the shims are the right thickness. If you've got everything right the mortice and tenon will slide together without forcing the prongs of the mortice apart but the unglued frame will stay together when you pick it up.

Open-slotted
mortice and tenon

Cutting the pins

Careful chiselling is required with this method

Mature elm trees have been in decline in Britain now for more than 50 years. The ravages of the fungus *Ceratocystis ulmi* – better known to its enemies as Dutch elm disease – has brought down most specimens with a trunk more than 300mm (about 1ft) in diameter. On the waney edges of my wide boards, just under the bark, were tell-tale patterns of the galleries in which the elm-bark beetles had hatched their fungus-carrying brood.

Hand-planed boards

The planer in my workshop is only 10in wide, so was not relevant to my plans. Although my wood supplier has a planer wide enough to take the boards, I was worried that its hard-worked blades would tear at the wild grain around the knots, leaving them pitted.

So, I set to work with a hand plane on the sawn surfaces, accepting that I would have to hone the blade frequently because of the abrasive nature of elm. The top surface came successfully from a single board of full width and thickness. The pieces I selected for the sides and base had a tiny bit of cupping to be removed, so I ripped and jointed them before planing flat.

Carcass construction

With so many dovetail joints on the carcass corners, I find it's difficult to force them together if they are tight, yet the slightest gaps would be very conspicuous. For normal dovetails, on drawer sides and the like, I usually knife-mark the top of the pins from the underside of the tails. Sadly, there's no way I could cut the required accuracy through inch-thick dovetails using this technique. Instead I had to work out the following method so the visible surfaces would be marked directly off

one another.

Having prepared the faces, edges and ends of the four boards and chosen the front edges, mark out the dovetail pins on the ends of the carcass sides with a 1:8 guide. With 29 pins and 30 tails into the 660mm (26in) depth, the pitch of the pins works out at just less than 25mm (1in). In keeping with the Arts and Crafts style, the alternate pins are cut to ⅔ depth to enhance the visual interest of the joints. Mark these out with a knife-edged marker gauge on the end grain and after cutting all the pins full size, pare back alternate pins to the line.

For marking the tails, the carcass side is clamped to the left-hand end of the bench with pins protruding above the bench surface. The corresponding carcass, top or base, is lightly scribed twice with the marker gauge for two depths of pins, laid along the bench

'This cabinet uses internal pivot pins to avoid the look or feel of door hinges protruding from the front of a cabinet'

If you can make your joints fit your chisels it helps!

Intriguing figure and joint construction

Cutting drawer dovetails

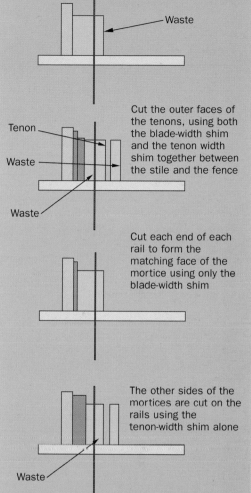

DOOR FRAME JOINTS

A bandsawn open-slotted mortice and tenon

Adjust the fence to make the deepest cuts on each end of the stiles. These will form the inner surfaces of the tenons. The fence stays in this position for the following cuts

Waste

Cut the outer faces of the tenons, using both the blade-width shim and the tenon width shim together between the stile and the fence

Tenon

Waste

Waste

Cut each end of each rail to form the matching face of the mortice using only the blade-width shim

The other sides of the mortices are cut on the rails using the tenon-width shim alone

Waste

and butted up to the side piece then clamped up tight against the pins using the tail vice. Next, use a square to mark from all four corners of each pin to the scribed lines where the tail will be cut. Cut the tails in the conventional way, by checking with a calliper they'll be a good fit on the pins.

The shoulders of the tails on the inside of the cabinet can be slightly chamfered to help the pins enter their sockets. Provided the chamfer is very small, it helps you spot any potential tightness when you first introduce the pins to the tails as a rehearsal for assembly.

When satisfied all the dovetail corners are good, the front and rear cross-shaped frames need to be made up with halving joints between the horizontal and vertical members, then double tenons cut where each end will enter the carcass. The corresponding through-mortice is again marked, then

cut from the outer surface to guarantee a clean gap-free joint. Kickers and runners for the drawers are made with dry-jointed tenons into mortices to allow for movement.

Glue-up

Gluing up any carcass can be a scary business, but with 120 dovetails and four double-tenon joints all coming together at once, good planning and slow-setting glue are essential.

Stand the cabinet sides on the base with the 58 lower pins loosely engaged in the chamfered entries to their sockets, while gluing the tenons of the horizontal frame into mortices in the side panels. Then bring the side panel mortice and tenons together with sash clamps. Next, glue the halving joint and lay the carcass top on the 58 upper dovetail pins so they are engaged loosely in their chamfered sockets.

Now all the carcass joints – dovetails and upper and lower tenons – should be lined up ready to be clamped together vertically. Use an artist's brush to glue the joint surfaces of all the pins swiftly, then pull the whole thing together with cramps between top and base. I use two sash cramps and a trusty pair of old canvass band clamps, at the same time dashing around with a large square and pulling the carcass up square by small movements of the clamp heads. The workshop was quite cool that day and the operation probably took about half an hour. I don't like to apply too much pressure with cramps, but with so many joints soaking up moisture from the glue it certainly took more force than usual. I must admit that if I were trying that operation again I would ask someone to help. After the glue sets, you can expose the clean pattern of the joints with a sharp plane.

'The carcass of this cabinet sits upon a pair of fairly massive pedestals . . . undercut to form front and rear feet, and with stepped fronts'

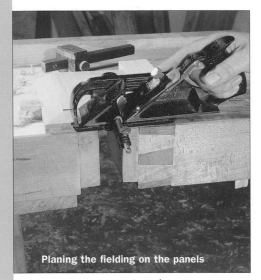

Planing the fielding on the panels

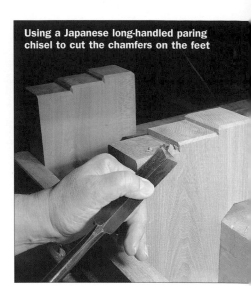

Using a Japanese long-handled paring chisel to cut the chamfers on the feet

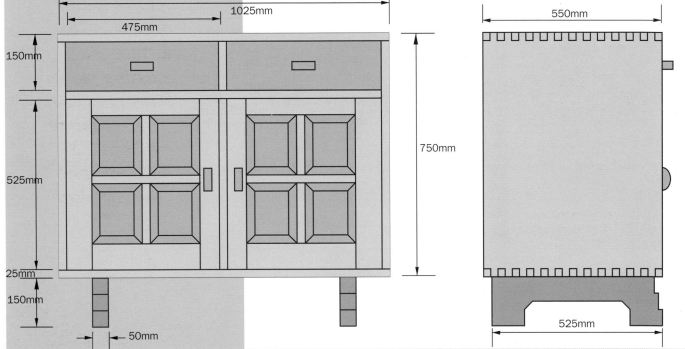

Look, no hinges!

This cabinet uses internal pivot pins to avoid the look or feel of door hinges protruding from the front of a cabinet. These doors are hung on pivot pins made from large brass screws that pivot in washers trapped in holes in the carcass. Variations on this method have served me well for a number of years. When I first made these simple hinges I thought I could claim it as a new idea, until I saw a similar method on a 17th-century chest – and it was still bearing up well!

First the doors are planed to fit their openings snugly, then a 1.5mm (¹⁄₁₆in) pilot hole is drilled through the carcass base and horizontal rail in the hinge position 25mm (1in) in from the carcass side and half the door thickness

in from the carcass front. With the door held in position – I wedged it with paper on all four sides – push a needle through each pilot hole to mark the door edge. With correct alignment this will be halfway through the tenon, and about 20mm (²⁵⁄₃₂in) from the end of the rail. The pilot hole can now be enlarged inside the opening to give clearance of the screw shaft, outside the opening to give a tight fit for the stack of brass washers. It's important that the pin pivots in the stack of trapped washers, not in the wood.

Drill the door frame and dry-fit the parts for a trial assembly. If all is well the frame can be removed, then you can plane it to allow for clearance and re-fit. The doors must have bevelled edges so they clear the cabinet frame and should

swing freely through an angle of about 120°, giving excellent access to the cabinet. Finally, plug the open hole with beeswax.

Finish

To make a simple back, vertical strips of cedar of Lebanon are sprung into slots in the top and base. All the cabinet faces are sanded with fine paper only to preserve the hand-planed surfaces and sharply defined mitred edges. Give all the outside faces four applications of Danish oil, brushed off then wiped off again, diluted with turpentine in ratios 1:1, 1:2, 1:3 then 1:4, sanding finely between each. Bring the finish to a sheen with beeswax and turpentine polish; I recommend it to my clients for future maintenance to help develop a patina. ■

Brendan Devitt-Spooner is a former teacher who turned to furniture-making and design in 1987. Largely self-taught, he takes a delight in using solid wood and has a preference for English timber

PHOTOGRAPHY BY ANTHONY BAILEY
ILLUSTRATIONS BY IAN HALL (MAIN)
AND SIMON RODWAY

Based on an earlier concept, **Brendan Devitt-Spooner** makes a display cabinet

'Pieces for exhibitions can be a wonderful way for a craftsman to realise a new design or to further an existing piece. They can also be stressful or exhilarating, depending on how you view them'

Spoonerism

Pieces for exhibitions can be a wonderful way for a craftsman to realise a new design or to further an existing piece. They can also be stressful or exhilarating, depending on how you view them. Like most makers I experience both feelings. I love the thought of making something new and showing it off but I also find the exhibition itself always starts too early; necessitating working into the night although not through it – yet!

The inspiration for this piece came from making a cabinet the previous year for a client. I enjoyed the overall feel of the cabinet – both metaphorically and physically – and decided to evolve the concept to a larger piece. I don't know about the rest of the cabinetmakers out there but I don't always draw things on paper, particularly when they are speculative pieces. I just trust my luck and judgement and go for it!

Timbers
I liked the timbers I'd used in the previous piece and so decided I would continue with the oak (*Quercus* sp) and walnut (*Juglans* sp) mix. The oak for the sides and doors was quarter-sawn. I also used cedar of Lebanon (*Cedrus libani*) for the rear panels and drawer bases. Sycamore (*Acer pseudoplatanus*) was used for drawer sides.

Main carcass
The main carcass is simply two sides joined together by the base, drawer carcass and top rails. Rather than have flat sides I decided to continue the technique employed on the earlier cabinet and use flutes. It's a very tactile feature and quite easy to execute. Each side is six pieces of oak 1500 by 62.5 by 30mm (59 by 2½ by 1⅛in) machined up – slightly oversize – and left to settle for a while. Taken to the final dimension each piece is then fluted – through a spindle moulder. Lay out the single pieces into completed sides. It's also worth spending a little time selecting the two most attractive pieces for the front.

Top

The top is simply three pieces of oak, loose-tongued and glued but remember the grooves are stopped! After cleaning up, the ends are marked out with a concave curve, sawn on a bandsaw and cleaned again with a compass plane. A small chamfer is run around all edges before being fixed to the carcass with brass countersunk screws.

Handles

I always seem to leave the design of handles to last. I like to see the job in the flesh before finally choosing them. There wasn't much to decide really. I liked the ones I'd put on the earlier cabinet except this time I made them from walnut rather than oak. The curves in the vertical ones are formed by holding them against a small sanding wheel held in the drill press and the curves in the horizontal ones by holding against the wheel of the pad sander. All the handles are attached by brass screws from inside the doors and drawers.

Drawers

The drawers are totally conventional with oak fronts, sycamore sides to accentuate the dovetails and cedar bottoms.

Doors

Construction is straightforward. The 8mm (⁵⁄₁₆in) grooves for holding the panels are made using a spindle moulder. However, after cutting out the curves on the top rails, most of the groove will have disappeared. Using a bearing-guided slot cutter the groove is now formed around the profile. The rebate which holds the central flute on the face of the doors is formed using a rebating cutter in a router. The central flute hides the gap between the doors and provides a central vertical focal point. Ideally, this would be made using the appropriate spindle cutter. I did not have one. What I did have was a wooden moulding plane.

Top rails

These are dovetailed into the top. Rather than form the dovetail the whole thickness of the rail I created a ledge about 5mm (³⁄₁₆in) short. This allows the rail to be cramped into place while scribing the dovetail on the end.

Interior carcass

Essentially, this was a simple carcass from 17mm (¹¹⁄₁₆in) thick oak having two outside compartments and one larger one in the middle. The corners are all through-dovetailed and the dividers stopped housed. I could have dispensed with the back but then anything small may have fallen between the carcass and the cedar panels of the main carcass back. However, I decided to have a separate back for the smaller carcass but did not want it to clash with the main one. With careful measuring the two backs look as one when viewed from the front with all doors open. The top carcass is held to the sides of the main carcass with four 25mm (1in) No. 10 screws on each side. The doors are constructed in the same way as the larger ones.

Plinth rail

The front, although using the same joint, is fluted. The depth of the flute is up to the maker. Mine are determined by the availability of a suitable radius and they're cut out using a bandsaw, cleaned up using a compass plane and sanded. These two rails can be glued into position while the rest of the carcass is still cramped up.

Sides

Each side is six pieces of oak 1500 by 62.5 by 30mm (59 by 2½ by 1⅛in) machined up – slightly oversize – and left to settle for a while. Taken to the final dimension each piece is then fluted – through a spindle moulder. Lay out the single pieces into completed sides.

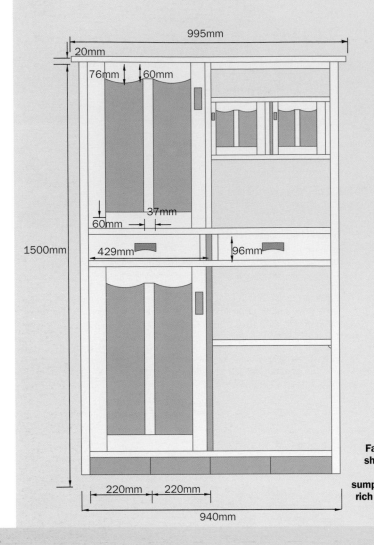

995mm

20mm

76mm 60mm

37mm

60mm

1500mm

429mm 96mm

220mm 220mm

940mm

Face on showing the sumptuous rich figure

After marking each piece in pencil with a code, so they can be realigned later, each one is grooved to accept a loose tongue – in this case 6mm (¼in) birch (*Betula* sp) ply. After a dry run to ensure no piece of ply is too wide – not a good thing to discover when gluing is under way – each side is glued. Be careful with the peaks of the flutes, they're easily knocked, and ensure the sash cramps are alternately positioned on each side to aid flatness and leave to dry. The base and the main shelf are made up of three boards again loose-tongued and then re-machined to thickness. At this stage you'll also need the two top rails, the drawer rails and guides and the two bottom rails, one of which is walnut.

Marking out

When the sides are dry, the flat side of each can be cleaned up. This may be determined by the availability of equipment. In my workshop I have a 16in (405mm) surfacer which produces the desired result.

With both boards clamped flat, side to flat side, check they're parallel and

carefully trim the ends to length. At this stage the rebates to contain the rear frame are made, using a bearing-guided rebate cutter in a portable router. Note the rebates do not extend to the end. I sanded the two flat sides before commencing any marking out.

The initial marking out consists of two stopped housings for the base and the main shelf and twin mortices for the drawer rails. With these cut out, chiefly using a router, the male parts on the mating pieces are formed. At this point the cabinet can be dry-assembled. To introduce pressure to the sides, enabling the housings to close up, a male caul was needed. I made mine from cheap, soft pine from a large DIY store.

Backed with something a little more substantial, the carcass was cramped together and the two top rails can now be made. These are dovetailed into the top.

Rather than form the dovetail the whole thickness of the rail I create a ledge about 5mm (³/16in) short. This allows the rail to be cramped into place while scribing the dovetail on the end.

More carcass

When marked, the carcass is disassembled and the sockets cut out. Great care must be exercised over the flutes. When working on the flat sides I use thick cardboard to cushion. The dovetail slots below the base can also be formed in the sides using a router and dovetail cutter. Returning to the drawer rails, the remaining parts of the assembly can now be completed. To enable the centre flute running through the centre of the cabinet to continue past the drawers, separate the two drawers by two vertical dividers twin-tenoned top and bottom. The runners are tenoned into the front and back rails but are left short and not glued. The two guides are dry-tenoned into the two front dividers and positioned at the rear with a screw. There's one divider to the rear.

The last part, before the finishing, is the marking out and drilling of holes for the lower shelf supports and drilling the holes in the top rails for attaching the top. As with most carcasses it's easier to clean up and finish the insides before gluing. Remember to mask off the joints

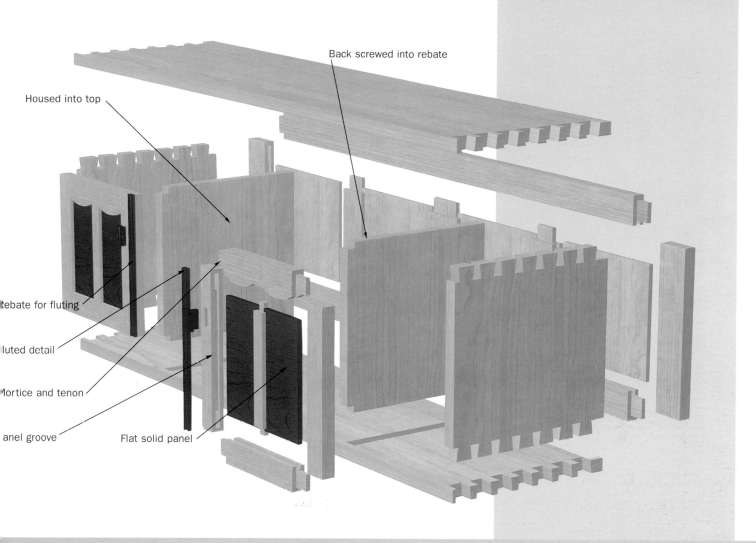

Back screwed into rebate

Housed into top

Rebate for fluting

Fluted detail

Mortice and tenon

Panel groove

Flat solid panel

and pay particular attention to the woodwork surrounding and guiding the drawers. All this must be beautifully smooth and wax-finished.

Glue-up

Having ensured all the components fit together, arrange all the sash cramps and scrap wood ready for a methodical and unhurried gluing operation. Once complete, check for squareness and leave to dry. At this stage the two lower rails can be worked on, the rear one is simply a piece of oak with dovetailed tongues. The front, although using the same joint, has a fluted front. The depth of the flute is up to the maker. Mine are determined by the availability of a suitable radius and they're cut out using a bandsaw and cleaned up using a compass plane and then sanded. These two rails can be glued into position while the rest of the carcass is still cramped up.

Back frame

The next major component is the back frame, while preventing your worldly treasures falling out of the back,

maintains the rigidity of the whole. Quite simply, the frame is made up from 20mm (2¾in) thick oak and grooved on all edges housing a cedar panel. The joints are all mortice and tenon and cedar of Lebanon is used for the panels. Before gluing up the frame the panels are finished with Vaseline. This maintains the low lustre and still allows the smell to emanate.

Gluing up is straightforward, apart from the mid rails, which need a scrap filler placed on either side of the centre panel to allow the sash cramps to exert pressure along the whole length. I always try and leave gluing up the backs until the end of the day. Although they're light in themselves, when loaded with cramps they're almost impossible to move.

The following morning, after removing all the cramps, the back frame can be cleaned up. Unless you have the luxury of a large bench, with access all the way round, this operation is sometimes more easily done on the floor. With a finely set plane, proceed around all the joints planing at 45° and then

sand the whole. This is left while the main carcass is cleaned up on its front and back sides. The frame can now be fitted to the carcass. I find this whole operation easier if the carcass is on the ground. Lay the frame along one edge and note where – or if – the bottom needs any taking off to form a right angle. The other long side can now be planed until it fits snugly. I leave the top edge until after the frame has been screwed in. With the carcass up the wrong way the bottom edges of the carcass can be cleaned up. A small chamfer is run along all the edges to prevent breakout when it is moved over carpets etc.

At this point the outside edges of the cabinet are cleaned up. A block of softwood shaped to the correct curvature is made and then all the flutes are hand sanded – this also removes any glue excesses and slight irregularities between the peaks.

The top is simply three pieces of oak, loose-tongued and glued but remember the grooves are stopped! After cleaning up, the ends are marked out with a

The interior

The back

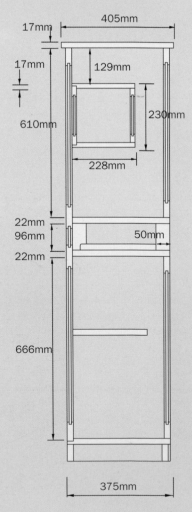

The back off, with cedar panels in interior carcass

concave curve, sawn on a bandsaw and cleaned again with a compass plane. A small chamfer is run around all edges before being fixed to the carcass with brass countersunk screws.

Doors

The doors on this cabinet are the first thing most people notice when viewing it. Because the curves are the 'wrong' way up they become a feature. Like most panelled doors the construction is straightforward. The 8mm (⁵⁄₁₆in) grooves for holding the panels are made using a spindle moulder. However, after cutting out the curves on the top rails, most of the groove will have disappeared. Using a bearing-guided slot cutter the groove is now formed around the profile. The panels for this cabinet came from a set of consecutive flitches taken from the base of an old tree.

At this point luck kicked into play. Without any crunching sounds coming from the thicknesser, all of them are thicknessed down to 8.5mm (just over ⁵⁄₁₆in) without any tearout. The remaining 0.5mm is removed on a pad sander. Considering the wild grain I was lucky. After oiling the walnut, the panels are fitted into the grooves and the doors glued up.

Once glued, the doors are cleaned up. The rebate, which holds the central

flute on the face of the doors, is now formed using a rebating cutter in a router. The doors are now fitted to the carcass using solid drawn, brass butts. The central flute hides the gap between the doors and provided a central vertical focal point. Ideally this would be made using the appropriate spindle cutter. I did not have one. What I did have was a wooden moulding plane. Although it was the wrong curvature I managed to remove most of the waste and cleaned it up with glasspaper over a curved wooden block.

With the other edges cleaned up the flutes are glued onto the right-hand doors. I don't know if there's any convention when deciding which door opens first but this way seemed right. Another small length of this fluting was tapped gently into the space between the drawer dividers.

Interior

With just the shelf and shelf supports to go into the lower part it is almost finished but every time I looked at it I felt there was something lacking. At this point I decided to include the upper carcass inside the top doors.

Finish

The whole cabinet is finished with three coats of Danish oil and rubbed back with Vaseline. ■

Tradition recaptured

Antique-inspired, this chest of drawers has clean and simple lines

Mark Applegate completed his MSc in Forest Products: Design and Manufacture at Hooke Park College before becoming a self-employed designer-maker

PHOTOGRAPHY BY STEPHEN HEPWORTH AND MARK APPLEGATE

ILLUSTRATIONS BY SIMON RODWAY

Mark Applegate

makes a five-drawer oak and sycamore chest

STEPHEN HEPWORTH

This traditional chest of drawers evolved from a photograph brought in by the client. His brief required a five-drawer chest, similar to the antique in the client's photograph. We decided upon French oak (*Quercus* sp) for the main carcass and drawers. Due to a budget limit, sycamore (*Acer pseudoplatanus*) stringing is used instead of boxwood (*Buxus*). To reduce cost further, the panels are left square and simple, instead of the originals, which were raised and fielded. The client the brass handles to best match the original. The top drawers are to have brass locks and keyhole – and to match similar furniture in the client's home, the chest needed to be stained.

Design parameters

The French oak planks are sorted into matching sets for the drawer fronts, panels, top and the best match on the stiles and rails. Any quarter-sawn planks are set aside for the drawers and top. This gives an overall integrity to the chest as regards the grain match and stability. To ensure an aesthetic continuity, the top two drawers are selected from the same plank of oak.

I machined the front and back drawer rails to 30mm (1⅛in) thick, as this gave a robust and solid look to the chest. The side rails and stiles are also kept a healthy 60mm (2⅜in) wide.

After machining the drawer components first, allowing a few millimetres to finish later, these are stacked and left to condition. Critical components that move, such as drawers, can then acclimatise to the desired humidity level.

Construction techniques

After being cooped up in dust mask, ear defenders and chained to the machines for a number of hours, I looked forward to some woodwork.

On symmetrical pieces, I usually create a rod on a piece of ply or MDF. On the chest, I set out the front and side sections. This, all things being equal, should ensure accurate marking out. I tackled the front, back rails and stiles

Drawers removed showing drawer frames and dividers

PHOTOGRAPH BY STEPHEN HEPWORTH

Drawer dovetails

Sycamore stringing

4mm (⁵⁄₃₂in) sycamore stringing about 50mm (2in) in from the stiles and rails gives a classic look to the oak panels. I purchased a 4mm (⁵⁄₃₂in) spiral router cutter to cut the groove in the panel, and I was pleased with the clean, sharp-edged grooves that this cutter produced. The router, used with the fence attachment, remains at the desired setting.

The sycamore plank for the stringing is thicknessed to a desired depth, in this case 10mm (⅜in). The board is then fed through the saw with the fence set at about 6mm (¼in) to produce strips. The thicknessing is a bit tricky as grain tearout on a piece does not make a neat stringing. To alleviate this I marked each piece with an arrow to denote grain direction. Then, placing each piece on a flat board – ply/block – I fed them into the thicknesser denoting the grain direction. As a further precaution I changed the planer blades. The finished machine thickness is just over 4mm (⁵⁄₃₂in), enough to sand into a tight fit into the groove.

At the corners, I mitred the stringing, using a marking knife and chisel, after cutting at 45˚ with a fine

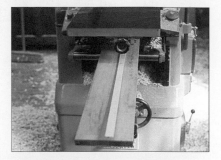

A ply board makes it safer and easier to plane up the thin stock of the stringing

Fitting the stringing on the drawer fronts

saw. Glue, a block of softwood, and a hammer ensured the stringing sat snugly in the grooves. A sharp plane, scraper and fine glasspaper flushed off the sycamore with the oak.

---

first – the front and back drawer openings should be the same to allow for an even drawer action with no binding.

The way I proceed is to transfer the marks off the rod onto one rail; collect the others together, G-cramp them to the first, and then transfer all markings. I transfer mortice and tenon shoulders with a marking knife.

Each rail/stile joint is a double mortice and tenon. Once the mortices are marked on all the stiles, I take every piece to the mortice machine, select the correct chisel, position the depth stop and plough through the lot in one go.

I cut the front and back double tenons by hand, taking care to chisel a clean shoulder. Then, after cutting the side tenons on the table saw, with the blade dropped down and a jig guard attached to the fence, the next operation is to prepare the rails for the drawer runners/kickers. These are morticed and tenoned to the rails, leaving a small

'This traditional chest of drawers evolved from a photograph brought in by the client'

allowance for movement on the rear shoulders; these allow the sides to move and are left dry.

By this time, there are numerous rails, stiles, runners and so on. I batched these up into component parts and set aside for sanding etc. Next, I embark on the side components. The basic construction of the stile/rail joint is a haunched mortice and tenon joint allowing for a groove for the panel.

I now had to consider the panels. Once machined, I book-match the boards and glue them together with biscuits. Next, I re-thickness the panels; then scrape and sand them. Finally, they are cut to size. The stiles and rails are grooved to receive the panel and the panel rebated on the inside face, to fit the groove.

The carcass consists of over 30

components and over 60 mortice and tenon joints. Therefore, gluing up the carcass has to be planned accordingly.

I started with the sides. The panel is spot-glued top and bottom, and the whole assembly is glued and cramped, checked for square and twist. Once the glue is set the sides are flushed off and sanded. These are now ready to receive the front and back rails.

Glue is spread quickly into all the mortices, then the rails pushed home and cramped. Checking for square with lots of sash cramps on the rails is not easy. However, as long as accuracy is maintained throughout, the piece should be true. I checked each joint with a square and made small adjustments as necessary on the cramps. It does help if the cramps are not over tightened as this

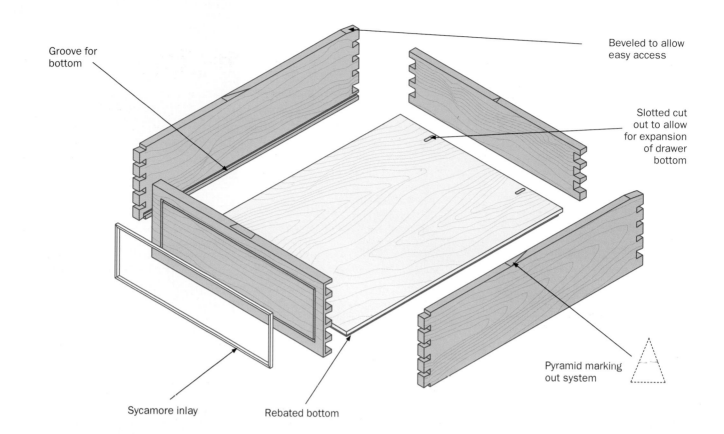

Groove for
bottom

Beveled to allow
easy access

Slotted cut
out to allow
for expansion
of drawer
bottom

Sycamore inlay

Rebated bottom

Pyramid marking
out system

**Moulding detail
on the top**

'*After being cooped up in dust mask, ear
defenders and chained to the machines for
a number of hours, I looked forward to
some woodwork*'

can tend to bow the rails. Generally, I glue
up on my bench as I know that it is flat
and, therefore, it's easy to check and
adjust for twist.

Next, I made the top, fitted the
stringing as before, routed a 10mm (⅜in)
cove around three sides, scraped and
sanded it and slot-screwed it onto the
top kickers. The top fitted snugly on the
carcass with a 10mm (⅜in) overhang
around three sides and 20mm (¾in) on
the rear. Having an overhang on the rear
of a free-standing piece means that the
top can touch the wall when the plinth is
against the skirting.

The carcass sits on a waisted plinth.
To construct the plinth, I mitred the front
and sides together, then morticed and

tenoned the rear rail. I bandsawed the
profile of the waisted plinth and cleaned
the edges with a sanding drum fixed to a
drill. To match the top, I routed a cove
around the three top edges. After gluing
the plinth together I added corner blocks
to give strength and screwed the plinth
to the carcass.

Drawer construction and techniques

Once the carcass is complete I can start
the drawers. I machined the components
to the desired size. The fronts are 20mm
(¾in) thick; the sides and backs 15mm
(⅝in). I machined the depths to just over
the size of the opening. I used the
pyramid pencil marking system to

denote a drawer component and placed
a number on the drawer to denote
position. This stops any confusion over
different drawer parts.

When tackling drawers I usually start
with the sides, checking the grain
direction, and orientate it towards the
rear of the carcass. This is because, when
planing the sides to fit, it is easier to plane
away from the front dovetails. Each
drawer side is parallel-planed to fit the
opening sides; the aim being to achieve
a tight fit that slides smoothly in the
opening.

I treat the front and back lengths as a
matching set, and they are cross-cut and
planed on the end grain to within a
finger push to the opening.

Once all the drawer parts are a good
fit – in their respective openings – I
groove each component, including the
back, on the table saw. In this example
I used an 8mm (⅜in) groove. It may
seem odd to groove the back but

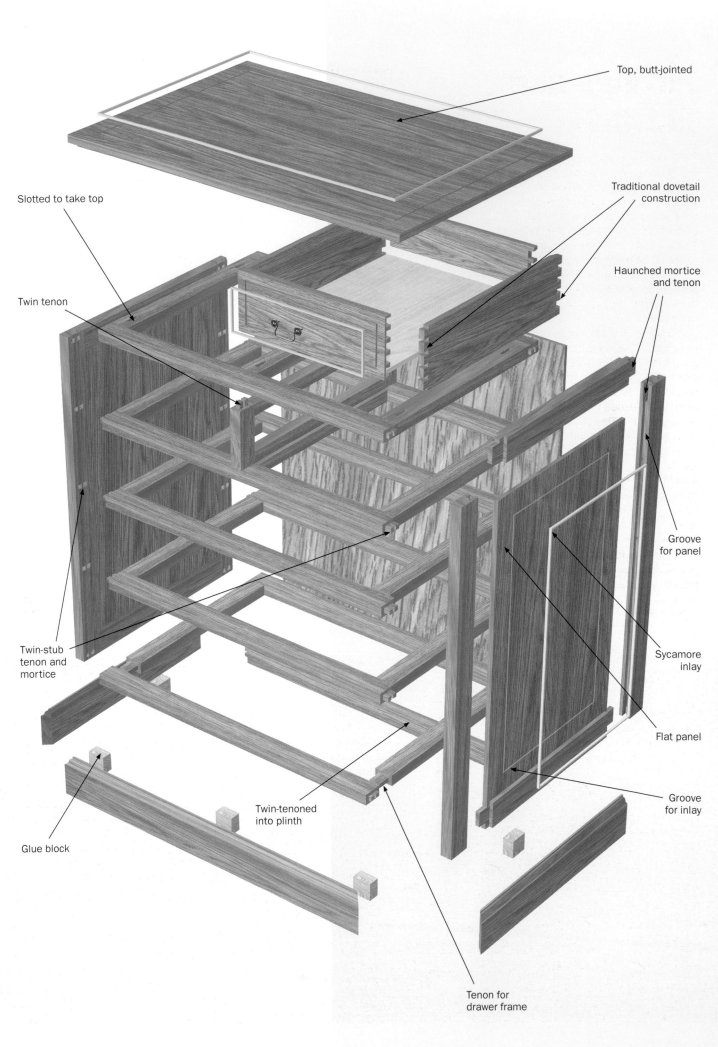

Top, butt-jointed

Traditional dovetail construction

Haunched mortice and tenon

Slotted to take top

Twin tenon

Groove for panel

Twin-stub tenon and mortice

Sycamore inlay

Flat panel

Twin-tenoned into plinth

Groove for inlay

Glue block

Tenon for drawer frame

Fittings and finishes

STEPHEN HEPWORTH

I fitted brass locks and keyholes to the top drawers and fitted the handles of the client's choice – oak handles would have been better. Cedar drawer bottoms are added to the drawers with a rebate on the underside. There was no need for slips, as the sides of the drawers are thick enough.

Finally, I fitted a cedar tongued-and-grooved back panel which is screwed to the corresponding rebate in the back of the carcass.

The whole of the carcass and drawers are given a final sand, finishing with 400-grit paper. The finishing treatment the client requested included staining. As I had already fitted the sycamore stringing I needed to prevent discolouration. This proved to be a bit of a headache but, finally, I masked around the stringing, applied a coat of wax to the stringing, and then stained the chest with Bichromium of Potash. Once dry, I Danish-oiled the chest, rubbing down between coats and, finally, waxed the whole piece.

I was a little apprehensive about the colour of the stain – I preferred the chest natural. However, once delivered and placed in its rightful resting place, it blended well with the other oak furniture in the room.

Traditional drawer construction with cedar bottom and slotted screws to allow for movement

remember that the back is the same depth as the sides at this stage. I now set the fence on the table saw to the top of the groove and pass the back through twice, flipping the back for the second cut. This will give a back depth that is above the groove and set down from the sides to reduce any vacuum effect.

The drawers are now ready for hand-dovetailing. I like to devote an uninterrupted time to dovetailing. One Friday afternoon I marked all the tails out, graduating the number to suit the different drawer sizes. This gave me a clear weekend to devote to dovetailing.

The other preparation I often do is to sharpen the saw and any chisels I need. Therefore, on Saturday morning I can begin the task straight away.

Cutting many dovetails is, I find, very much a state of mind. A relaxed and unhurried approach is preferable, and a steady rhythm of saw strokes and chisel paring soon makes light work of the pins. I saw all the pins first, cut out the waste with a coping or fret saw and then chisel the shoulders. I always use a marking knife for the shoulders and this line should never be breached. Do not, though, forget to cover the groove with a

tail on the front dovetails and start the dovetailing above the groove at the rear.

Now I'm ready to tackle the through pins on the backs. After aligning the backs upright in the vice, with the sides supported on a plane and placed sideways on the bench, the pins can be marked out. There are many ways to mark the pins and I still use a sharpened 4H pencil; others use marking knives, or the saw. Whilst sawing the pins I saw down the pencil line, leaving approximately a third of the pencil thickness. This should give a good, tight joint. I always try the dovetails for fit, but never hammer them home until I need to.

The pins on the lapped-front dovetails are a little more time-consuming. They are marked out the same way and the pins sawn. There are various ways of removing the waste – I use a router to cut

'When tackling drawers I usually start with the sides, checking the grain direction, and orientate it towards the rear of the carcass'

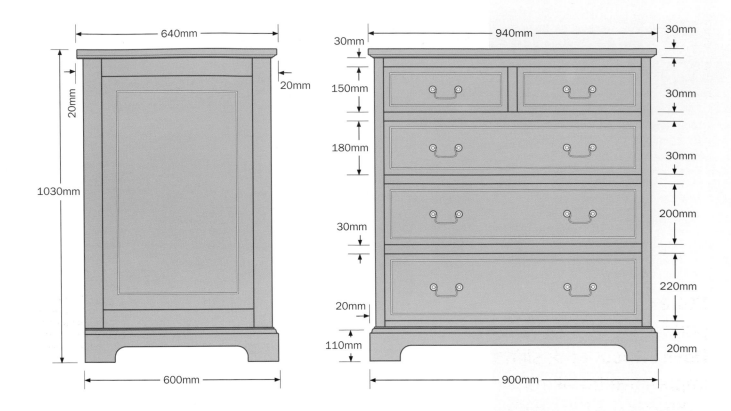

'Cutting many dovetails is, I find, very much a state of mind'

out most of the waste and then clean up with a sharp chisel. Most care is needed to ensure that the pin recesses are long enough. I use a cutting gauge to mark the desired lap and then slightly overcut them with the chisel by just a whisper.

The drawers needed stringing with sycamore to match the top and sides. The same method is followed as before, with a smaller margin. The main consideration is the keyhole location and this had to be a slight compromise.

Before gluing up, I mask off the dovetails, and wax the insides. This not only gives a good finish to the inside of the drawers, but also allows for easy removal of glue.

As long as care is taken with the execution of the dovetails, the only tools needed to glue them up are a hammer, block of wood, glue, a cloth and tape,

Stringing on side panel before the stain is applied

or lathe, for measuring the diagonals. I spread an even amount of glue onto the pins, align the dovetails and drive them home with the hammer and the block of wood. I tend to rotate the corners and hammer a bit at a time. I check for wind on the bench and measure the diagonals for square, and make any adjustments. Whilst curing, the drawers are set on a

flat and true surface to stop any twist or damage. The drawers can then be planed to fit the openings. If all goes well this should not take too long, and an even, slack-free slide obtained. I wax the runners etc to give a smooth action and inform the client that waxing the runners is a desired maintenance requirement. ■

Breakfront with tradition

State-of-the-art hi-fi demands pride of place – **Brendan Devitt-Spooner** designs an impressive breakfront cabinet for a big noise

Brendan Devitt-Spooner is a former teacher who turned to furniture-making and design in 1987. Largely self-taught, he takes a delight in using solid wood and has a preference for English timber

High-class craftsmanship designed to complement high fidelity

GMC/ANTHONY BAILEY

During the summer of 2000 (I think we had a dry day then!) a regular customer of mine called me over as he wanted a cabinet to fit into an alcove to house, among other things, a stereo, video tapes and glassware.

The stereo was a very upmarket CD player, which was quite minimalist and therefore would be situated in a prominent position. The glassware would be behind glazed doors, while the remaining items would be hidden from view behind panelled doors.

After an initial consultation to verify the dimensions of the space the cabinet was to occupy, the items that the cabinet had to contain, the position and proximity of power points, the size of the skirting board, etc., I spent the next week sketching different ideas before returning to the client for his views. After a little 'tweaking' the preferred option was chosen and I then made a detailed drawing for presentation, which was duly accepted.

Timber

The chosen woods were American cherry (*Prunus serotina*) for the whole, apart from wenge (*Millettia laurentii*) for the plinth, inlays and handles, quartered English oak for the drawer sides and cedar of Lebanon for the drawer bases and the cabinet backs.

One of the pleasant things about American cherry, as well as the other American timbers, is that they enter the UK square-edged and therefore have little waste. However, one must be aware that under American grading rules sapwood is not necessarily a defect and one must expect to find 'some' in a pack. Although not a defect, the sapwood is a different colour and I did not want to have any, or certainly not much, showing. With careful positioning I found it possible to utilise all the timber. Components like the rear frame members could contain a surfeit of sapwood without detriment to the overall piece.

Lower cabinet

The lower cabinet is actually made up from three smaller units, which are screwed together to form the whole.

Making the plinth

The plinth is designed to stand at 75mm (3in) high to match the surrounding skirting boards. Due to a scarcity of wenge, I made the plinth up in cherry (some of the sappy stuff) and then veneered it with sawn-cut wenge. The plinth is joined at the corners with tongue-and-groove joints and with through-housing joints at the front (see drawing). Before gluing up, slots were cut in to house the buttons. This could be ignored if expansion plates were going to be used instead. Fortunately I already had some 2mm ($\frac{5}{64}$in) thick wenge veneer. After gluing up and cleaning up the top and bottom surfaces the front and side surfaces were veneered. After cutting to size and then sanding, the veneers were glued in sequence to the plinth. With careful use of a chisel all the end-grain was trimmed and finally cleaned up. The whole plinth was then finished with Danish oil and put aside.

Attention can now return to the carcasses. These need to be cleaned up. I use a jointer plane, which is particularly useful when doing the front and back edges, as it is long enough to straddle corners to maintain flatness. These edges can now be sanded before the three carcasses are screwed together. Insert the screws from inside the central carcass – much easier than the smaller ones! When joining the three cabinets it is a good idea to sit them on a known flat surface and G-clamp them together. This way you can ensure that there will be no awkward inaccuracies when coming to fit the plinth and top. Before fitting the plinth, give the underside of the base a coat of oil or whatever finish you prefer.

Corner of the glass door section showing the detailing, the chamfer and the inlay on the top

The cove on the underneath of the top

The two outside ones are simple carcasses with no internal fitting. The centre cabinet, however, contains the necessary woodwork to hold two drawers. All three carcasses have a common plinth and top.

Begin by making up all the sides and bases for each carcass. As the bases for the two outside carcasses are quite short I decided to make them as one long one and then after machining to cut it into the two. All the components were grooved on a spindle moulder fitted with a ¼in grooving cutter. Using birch ply, which is a generous 6mm (approx ¼in), all the sides were made up, cramped and left to dry. At this point all the other rails for the carcasses can be machined.

Dry sides and bases can be resurfaced and thicknessed and then sanded prior to dimensioning. For joining the sides to the bases I used a tongue-and-groove joint. I like the way most of the joint has the timber of one component inside the other. With all three carcasses joined, I formed a rebate on the inside edge of each. Usually I make the rebates half the thickness of the timber and about 22mm (⅞in) wide. At this point the top rails and drawer support rails etc. can be jointed. This is all basic cabinetwork with single lap dovetails for the top rails and twin mortice and tenons for the lower rails and vertical dividers.

The drawer runners are loose-tenoned to allow for the movement of the carcasses. The top rails need to have countersunk holes to allow the top to be screwed down to the carcasses. As with all work involving drawers, the accuracy with which the carcass and associated woodwork is done is most important. Spend time checking and double-checking before cutting. At this stage the two mortices that will hold the drawer stops can be cut – it is somewhat difficult to do this after gluing! As the carcasses will all have loose shelves the holes for adjusting them need to be drilled. After all the preparation has been done the inside faces of each side and base and most sides of the drawer rails can be polished. Finally, after checking all is well, the three carcasses can be glued up. Ensure everything is 'square' and set aside while you begin on the plinth.

Three carcasses

With all three carcasses together, the plinth can now be fitted using buttons. The next stage is to make up the top. As with most pieces of furniture the top is

DRAWINGS BY SIMON RODWAY
ILLUSTRATION BY IAN HALL

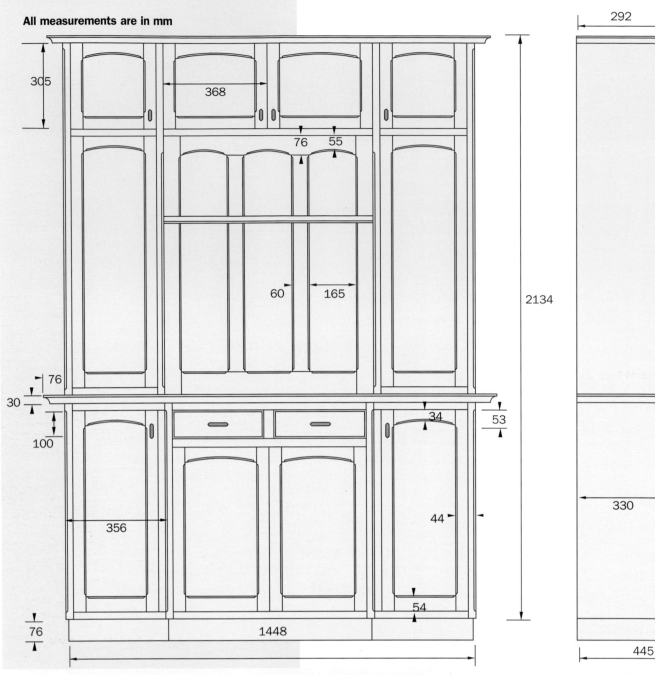

All measurements are in mm

one area where careful selection of timber can make all the difference to the finished piece. As the top is breakfronted it can be made initially as two pieces – the larger back and the smaller front. By making them separately the edge where the small piece fits to make the whole can be pre-finished as well as the ends of the smaller piece. All pieces were joined together using birch loose tongues that stopped 40mm (1⅝in) from the ends. After gluing, this was then machined again and sanded. The ends were trimmed to length before a bearing-guided cove cutter was used to form the profile. It was at this point that crisis design kicked in. The bearing cutter followed the edge faithfully producing an accurate shape. The problem was that it would not produce a sharp mitre on an internal corner. When no obvious

solution appeared, the only option left was to go to work with a gouge. If you have tried this you know how difficult it is. If you haven't, try Plan B. This involves keeping the two parts separate, moulding all edges and then mitring the front into the larger piece. With the mitres fitting, the two parts can be grooved to accept a loose tongue and glued together. Whichever route you take the next stage will be to fix the top to the carcasses.

Top to bottom

Ensure the top is central and square to the carcass before drilling holes. Again it is a good idea to G-clamp the top in place while marking the holes – don't forget the scrap wood! With the lower carcass finished, the inlays in the top can be worked. This was done using a 2mm

straight cutter in a router. Part of the operation can be done using a fence; however, guides will be needed to be cramped to the top to complete the grooves. Using a chisel the rounded corners can be squared. The inlays are from wenge. These were made by thicknessing a piece to 4mm (⁵⁄₃₂in) and then bandsawing the small strips slightly wider than the grooves. Careful planing brought the strips to a slightly tapered cross-section. Before they can be fitted the ends have to be mitred. With a little glue, the strips are gently knocked in using a pin-hammer and a block of softwood. The resulting protrusions were removed using a scraper and then sanded. Normally at this stage of making a cabinet I would move on to the rear frames. However, as this cabinet has a top which also has rear frames I decided

Cedar of Lebanon back panel in the top section

Quarter-sawn oak drawer sides and cedar bottoms, traditional materials of the best makers, with modern wenge handles

Adjustable solid shelf on the inside of the cupboard

it would be prudent to complete all the carcasses and then make all the rear frames as the machining time would be reduced due to only one set-up.

The upper case

The upper case comprises two tall 'tower' units and a connecting cabinet joining both towers at the top. The two towers are quite simple constructions involving tongue-and-groove joints at the bottom, stopped housings at the fixed shelf point and dovetailed rails at the top. The connecting cabinet is similarly constructed, except that the sides are dovetailed to the base and that the sides do not come to the front of the carcass. They are stopped short by the thickness of the door plus 2mm ($\frac{5}{64}$in) (space taken up by the magnetic catch). This improves the appearance by removing the double

thickness of carcass, which would occur left otherwise. The two main parts of the towers have glass shelves and are adjustable, therefore sets of holes need to be drilled before all the internal faces are polished. Situated below the 'connecting' cabinet there is an arched rail.

This is morticed into the sides of the towers. Before the three become one these mortices need to be cut. After gluing and cleaning up, the cabinets are fixed together with 1½in No. 10 brass countersunk screws. Do not forget to include the arched rail. One small screw from inside the top carcass secures the centre of the arch. The upper cabinet can now be lifted onto the base – put some cloth, or whatever, on the base top to prevent any damage. With the upper cabinet sitting in its correct position, the two carcasses were secured by drilling a

hole up through the lower top into the upper base on each side and inserting a 1½in No. 10 brass screw. The rear frames can now be made. There are seven in total – six having cedar of Lebanon panels and the exposed one in the middle of the upper case which has cherry panels.

As would be expected, they are constructed using square-haunched mortice and tenons for all corners and stub mortice and tenons for the intermediate joins. The panels, which were all book-matched, sit unglued in 6mm ($\frac{1}{4}$in) grooves. After gluing and finishing, the frames are secured in the rebates of each carcass with 1¼in No. 6 brass countersunk screws. With the upper carcass the 'middle' cherry panelled rear frame has to be fitted first by screwing in from the adjacent rebates.

The middle exposed back panels are in cherry and the interior panels are in cedar. Again, the interior lighting adds a warm glow to complement that of the cherry

This prevents any other woodwork showing in the area occupied by the hi-fi. Two other tasks to be done are the drilling of four holes, which take brass rods for supporting the shelf over the hi-fi and the cutting of two 55mm (2⅛in) diameter blind holes for the low-voltage lighting units in the base of the upper connecting cabinet. Apart from the doors, the top for the upper carcass can be prepared and fitted. It is similar to the lower top apart from the breakfront. It is secured with 1¼in x 8s.

Doors

Traditional haunched mortices and tenons are used for the doors – square-haunched for the panelled doors and long- and short-shouldered for the glazed doors. Spend time in choosing the timber for the panels. The doors are hung using 2in solid drawn butts and kept secured with small magnetic catches.

Door-making is comprehensively covered in most woodworking books and therefore I will not dwell upon it here.

Drawers

Drawers were again constructed in the traditional way. Lapped dovetails for the fronts and through-joints for the back. The solid bottoms were grooved into the sides.

Handles

The shape chosen was based upon the shape of the door frames. They were made from wenge and fitted to the doors by two screws from inside the door.

Shelves

The timber shelves are simply made by using quartered stuff and joining them together with loose tongues.

The glass shelves were 6mm and polished on all edges.

Finishing

I am a great fan of Danish oil and will generally use three coats, applying each with a brush and wiping off as soon as it is absorbed, leaving at least a day between each coat to harden off properly.

I then finish with petroleum jelly, applying with wire wool. This achieves a gentle, understated shine. This is a tip that I picked up from Alan Peters' book *Cabinetmaking –The Professional Approach*, sadly out of print now, but well worth scouring the second-hand bookshops for. ■

Labour for love

PHOTOGRAPHY BY ANTHONY BAILEY   ILLUSTRATIONS BY SIMON RODWAY

Phillip Gullam makes a traditional dresser as a wedding gift

● **After leaving school in 1986, Phillip Gullam trained at David Armstrong Furniture in rural Somerset, and now works for a company in Loughborough**

When a close friend of mine got married, I decided to make a display cabinet for their kitchen. As it was quite a small room my first concern was to design a piece that wasn't too large and overbearing for the confined area, but at the same time was not so small as to be insignificant.

Design

My design originates from several pieces that I had seen in sale rooms. I wanted to recreate a traditional cabinet, which would fit well within their 150-year-old ex-miner's cottage. Having oak (*Quercus* spp) in mind for the cabinet, I made several unsuccessful trips to the timber yard before I found some excellent planks of brown oak lurking under a stack of uninspiring timber.

The cabinet carcasses are made up of six frames. The joints are traditional mortice and tenon with a simple bead on the inside edge.

Cutting

The first job is to carefully select the timber as you want to choose the right figure and colour for the areas of the cabinet most on show. Some of the pieces are changed around once machined, so it is advisable to have a few spares – they also prove useful for setting up on.

It is a good idea to work out the whole job in your head, or on a piece of paper, as there are quite a few different stages that need to be completed before gluing-up can take place.

When marking out the cutting

ABOVE RIGHT: Side panels – note beading on rails and sympathetic plinth and foot

RIGHT: Bottom door detail

list, be aware that where the front and side frames join, they need to look like a piece of 50 by 50mm, so try to arrange the grain so that the joint doesn't stick out like a sore thumb. The bases, top and panels are quite wide and need jointing. They should be glued at the start of the job so that they are ready when needed.

Once the timber is machined and marked out clearly, the mortices are

marked out and cut, and then the tenons. When cutting the joint, remember that 8mm (⁵⁄₁₆in), for the bead, will be cut off the mortices. Once the mortice and tenons have been cut, a 3.2 radius bead is cut on the inside edges, except for the top front frame. This has a separate bead that is put on later. I find the best way to avoid breakout when routing the bead is to set the cutter through a fence.

'The cabinet carcasses are made up of six frames. The joints are traditional mortice and tenon with a simple bead on the inside edge'

Mitres

Next, the mitres need to be cut – these should be done with care, otherwise the finished frame will have tight joints but open mitres. I cut my beads on a guillotine, but they can be done equally as well with a mitre template.

An 8mm (⅜in) groove is then run through the inside edge of the side frames for the panels. This is done on the cross-rails to form the shoulder, but should be stopped on the stiles. Once again, I find setting the cutter through a fence the best way to avoid breakout.

As I mentioned earlier, where the side frames join onto the front frame, the stiles are biscuited and glued. I find gluing them together at this stage means you can get even pressure along the whole joint.

Panels

Next come the panels; they are just plain panels with a rebate to make them flush on the back of the frame. They should be machined oversize at the start of the job, and made to their final dimension thickness once the groove has been cut in the rails.

The depth of the cut is 1 to 1.5mm (¹⁄₁₆in) more than the groove. The panels need to be 2 mm (¹⁄₁₆in) less on the height and 3mm (⅛in) less on the width. I set up the rebate cutter on one of the panels before I cut it to size.

It is best to sand the panels before cutting the rebate as sanding afterwards can cause a sloppy fit. To stop the corners looking too heavy, machine a 20mm (¾in) bevel, then carve a small scallop to neatly finish the ends – the scallop begins in line with the bead and is 25mm (1in) long – and then cut the depth of the bevel to stop any breakout when routing.

Once the bevel has been cut, use a ½in chisel to scallop down to the width of the bevel, but 3mm (⅛in) above it. The step should then be rounded-over using a sharp chisel.

The bottom doors are hinged with brass butt hinges which you can rebate out before gluing up – I used a jig for this.

A rebate is then cut in the back of the side frame stiles for the tongue-and-groove back. This is made about 1.5mm (¹⁄₁₆in) deeper than the tongue groove and half the thickness of the frame.

Before gluing up I find it easier to joint the frames for the top and bottom shelves – I use biscuits for jointing. I find it easier to get in with a biscuit jointer and cut the grooves at this stage, before the panels are in. The beads and edges are then sanded, and the side frames glued. Once these are set, clean the insides.

'…my first concern was to design a piece that wasn't too large and overbearing for the confined area, but at the same time was not so small as to be insignificant'

ABOVE: Handles and meeting stile detail

BELOW: Door open – note fielding on inside of the door panel

ABOVE RIGHT: Glass sliding doors are a neat way of saving space in a small kitchen

FEET

To stop the base looking too heavy, make small double bull-nose feet. The first bull-nose should go around the whole cabinet, and be 15mm (⅝in) bigger than the cabinet. The corners are mitred then glued. The second bull-nose comprises two corners and the back feet. The corners are two pieces, 70mm (2¾in) long, mitred together. Once the mitres are set, a 9mm (⅜in) roundover should be machined top and bottom. I find it best to do this on a router table and a fence. The pieces are then sanded and screwed in place.

Base

◄ The front frame is glued up next – it is best to do it this way to avoid the large frames having to be clamped on their sides. The top and bottom shelves are then cut to length, and a groove machined on both ends, so as to slide the shelf in on the biscuits. The front of the shelf and the frame also need to be biscuited. The base width is less the thickness of the rebate for the back.

Next, glue the base to the frames, making sure that any excess glue is wiped clean. You now have the base to the dresser, but it will still be unstable at the top of the back. A rail needs to be put in to make the whole structure rigid. For this, use a piece of 70 by 22mm (2¾ by ⅞in) oak with a 60mm (2⅜in) wide dovetail, 15mm (⅝in) long – the rail is also used for fixing the tongue-and-groove back.

Top

The top of the dresser is slightly different as it also has a top shelf – the same construction processes should be used for fixing these. The top shelf is flush with the top of the frame and the bottom shelf flush with the top of the bottom rail, as this is what the doors will slide onto.

Before gluing the shelves in, 3mm (⅛in) grooves need to be cut for the sliding doors (see diagram). The bottom shelf has a groove cut in it for plates to sit within.

The top and bottom shelves are then glued in.

Sliding doors

The dresser carcasses should now be pretty much completed. The doors are scribed mortice and tenon. Cut the tenons and scribe on a tenoner.

The stile profiles are then machined and finally the mortices are cut. The panels for the base doors are plain on the face and raised on the back. As the dresser is made to fit in a small space I wanted to keep the actual display area as large as possible, hence the sliding doors. As they will overlap, you only lose the width of a stile instead of two – not much, but enough to make a difference. The sliding doors also save having large glazed doors swinging out into a narrow kitchen.

Once the doors have been glued up, the base doors are fitted with a small gap around them of 1.5mm (⅟₁₆in) overall height and a fag-paper on the width. The top doors should be made 4mm (³⁄₁₆in) shorter over the height to allow for the rollers which

BELOW: Fig 1
The sequence
for cutting the
cornice

1 Cut V groove
2 Cut 45°
3 Cut 45°
4 Cut 45°
5 Plane

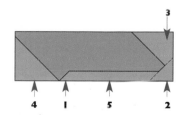

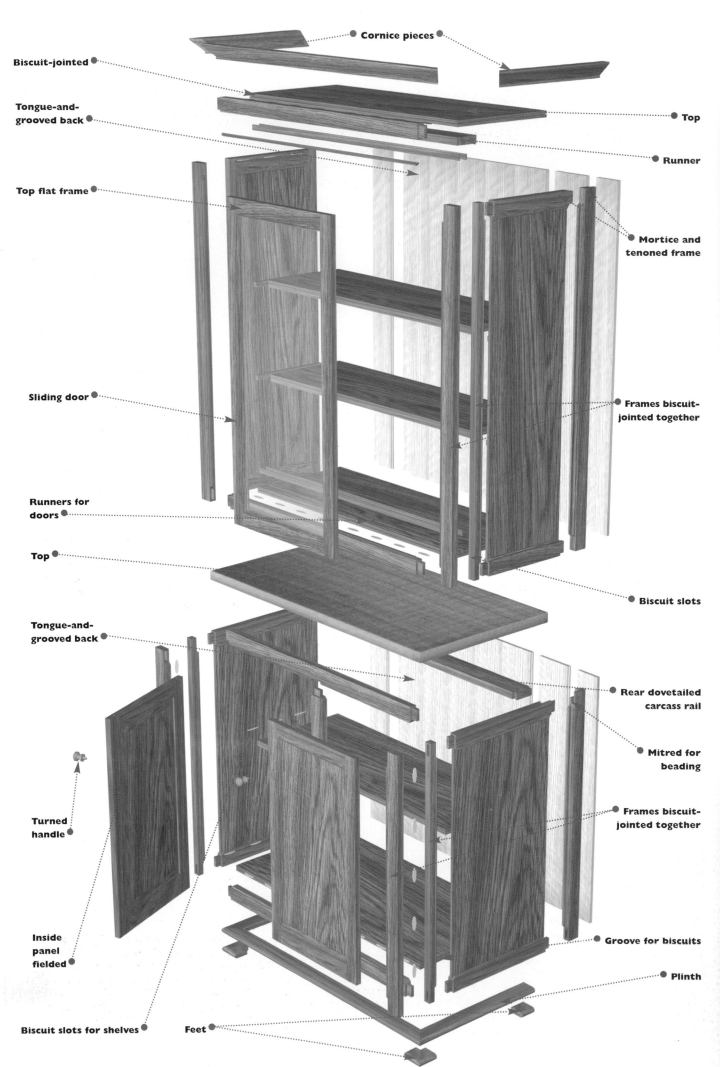

Cornice pieces

Biscuit-jointed

Top

Tongue-and-grooved back

Runner

Top flat frame

Mortice and tenoned frame

Sliding door

Frames biscuit-jointed together

Runners for doors

Top

Biscuit slots

Tongue-and-grooved back

Rear dovetailed carcass rail

Mitred for beading

Frames biscuit-jointed together

Turned handle

Groove for biscuits

Inside panel fielded

Plinth

Biscuit slots for shelves

Feet

ABOVE: Sliding door pull

ABOVE RIGHT: Cornice, scallop and bevel detail

BELOW: Dresser back, fitted into a rebate

BELOW RIGHT: Tongue-and-groove boarding in the back, from the inside

they slide on. As it is quite important to get the width right for the sliding doors, make up a full-size rod to ensure the sizes are correct. The right-hand door overlaps the left one by 50mm (2in) so all that can be seen of the right-hand stile of the left door, is the moulding.

Fitting doors

The doors are rebated after they have been glued up for the glass, using a flush trim cutter with a bottom bearing following the groove made with the stile moulding. They are then given small rollers to help

them slide more easily. Before they are fitted, the guides need to be made out of 3mm (⅛in) oak. The door should run smoothly along the guides – not bc tight at all.

They are then fitted – held in place by beading which is fixed separately onto the frame. The upright piece is wider as the left door goes behind it. Once everything is fitted and finished it should be fixed in place permanently, except for the top piece which is screwed in place so that, if necessary, the doors can be removed.

FINISHING

The cornice is made up out of 25mm (1in) timber (see Fig 1). Before the feet are glazed and magnetic catches are fixed, the whole dresser has three coats of 50:50 linseed oil and white spirit. The shelves have two coats of Danish oil to seal them. – this stops boxes of cereal soaking up the linseed oil. The oil takes a couple of weeks to dry completely, then the doors are glazed using 4.4mm toughened glass. Finally, the doors are hung and knobs and catches are fitted.

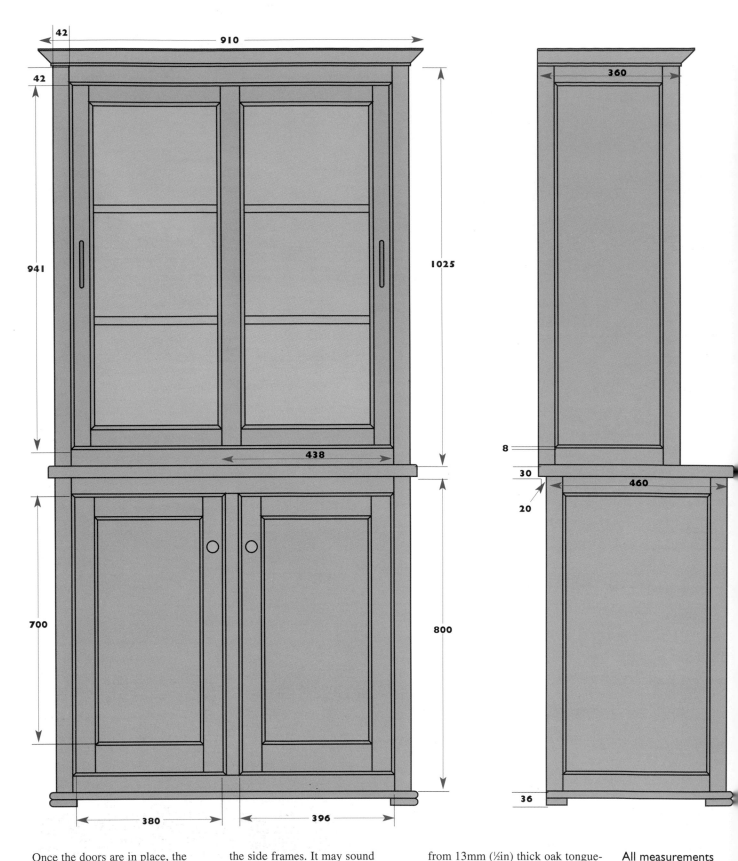

Once the doors are in place, the heights of the shelves should be marked. They are set so that the distance between the shelves is equal when you look through the glass but not when you open the door. The pulls in the doors are made using the same cutter as the plate grooves for the shelves.

Worktop

The shelves rest on the battens which are screwed and plugged to the side frames. It may sound obvious, but the shelf width has to be set just behind the innermost door.

The top of the dresser sits on an iroko (*Milicia excelsa*) worktop. It doesn't give you much working area but becomes a handy place to put mugs and glasses, ensuring nobody can open the doors and break a favourite. The top is fixed down with shrinkage plates through the frame at the front. The backs are made up from 13mm (½in) thick oak tongue-and-groove boards which are fixed in to allow for any movement.

Conclusion

My friends were over the moon with the cabinet as they at last had somewhere to put all their glassware that they received as wedding presents. I must admit, I was quite smug – no wedding list to ponder over and a chance to use one of my favourite timbers. ∎

All measurements are in millimetres

Upon retiring from the Metropolitan Police, David Kortright attended a course in fine cabinetmaking in Devon. Since then he has been making furniture at his workshop in Surrey, concentrating on commission work

David Kortright

makes a hi-fi cabinet
in English oak

PHOTOGRAPHY BY CHRIS SKARBON

My clients invited me down to their home in Surrey to see the surroundings in which the hi-fi cabinet they had commissioned would eventually live. The house was built around 1900 and has great character, and they were keen that any furniture for it should be sympathetic to these aesthetics.

The equipment to be housed in the cabinet consisted of three boxes – amplifier, tuner and CD player – and an impressive collection of compact discs. The speakers would stand separately. The piece was to be of English oak and would have the capacity to hold about 600 CDs. The dominant feature that I decided to take from the house was the arch effect used in its woodwork.

We discussed access to the controls and it was decided to have a door hinged at the top on pocket hinges so that it could slide into the carcass and out of the way.

Problems and solutions

I was really keen on this job because it had so much scope and a few adventures. I had never fitted a pocket hinge before, and as I was using it above the opening when it was designed to be used at the side, I was not sure whether this would be a problem. In the event it was not, and the mechanism worked perfectly in the horizontal plane.

Curved arches on the cabinet reflect the Gothic style of the client's house

Going Gothic

The next problem was that I wanted the door to slide right into the carcass. There is not much room between the top rail and the top of the door when it is slid away. My clients had selected some handles for the drawers which protruded too far out and would snag on the top rail so my solution was to use inset grips instead (see sidebar entitled *Handgrips*).

Arches

One of the most interesting features of this piece is the arched shape at the

Handgrips

Detail of the handgrip

Cut the bottom rail about 1mm (¹⁄₆₄in) oversize in all directions and then carefully cut it along its length 20mm (¾in) up from the bottom. Plane the sawn edges for a butt joint so that they could be re-glued. Rout two 100mm (4in) by 12mm (½in) grooves, 10mm (⅜in) deep, with a core box cutter, in the larger piece which will act as finger grips, and then glue the two pieces together again so that they look as if they have never been cut, hiding the two grooves in the joint.

Finish the rail to size. Using a piece of 9mm (⅜in) MDF, make a template to cut the grips 17mm (⅝in) deep into the rail using a short straight bearing-guided cutter.

The door folds away into the cabinet

Everything revealed

End panels

top of the side panels and the door at the front of the cabinet – this shape is also reflected in the plinth at the base. One point to watch here is that, having cut the curve and then mitred the point to fit into the stile, you have a sharp tip of oak that has cross-grain and threatens to break if you so much as breathe on it. My strategy is to cut the arch and then put the piece to one side until the final stages so that the cutting and fitting are done quickly, and the piece is not lying around the workshop waiting to get damaged.

Stiles

Next comes the stiles – the rails will be let into them 10mm (⅜in) and the mating edges must be perfect – and just to make life difficult, you cannot get a plane onto them. I use a table saw for this, setting the fence so that the distance between the fence and the blade, including the thickness of the blade, is 10mm (⅜in) short of the stile thickness. I then set the blade to maximum height to reduce the angle at the cutting edge. Even so, on my saw, a test cut showed that the saw cut 14mm (½in) further at the bottom of a 20mm (¾in) piece of timber than at the top.

After cutting the stiles the piece of waste is nipped off on the bandsaw, the saw cut is carefully trimmed with a sharp paring chisel, and the mitre is cut using a shop-made mitre jig.

Cutting mortices

Rout the mortices into both the stiles and rails, using a simple jig, and insert 12mm (½in) ply tenons which provide a perfect fit. Cut for three 40mm (1½in) mortices on each side of the top rail, the lower one nearly reaching the heel of the mitre. At this point you will find that the mortice will penetrate right through,

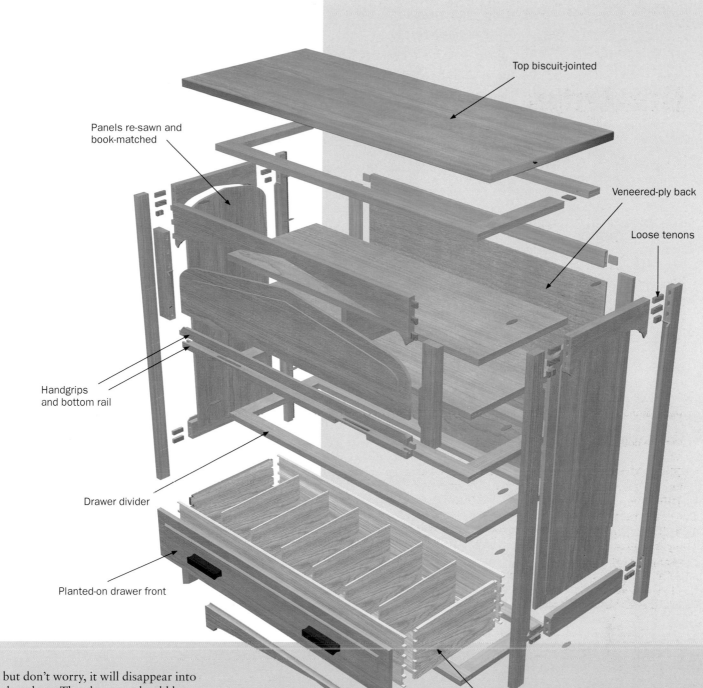

Top biscuit-jointed

Panels re-sawn and
book-matched

Veneered-ply back

Loose tenons

Handgrips
and bottom rail

Drawer divider

Planted-on drawer front

Plinth
glue blocks

Dovetail
construction

Plinth

but don't worry, it will disappear into
the rebate. The ply tenon should be
trimmed on the bandsaw so that it does
not protrude out from the mortice and
interfere with clamping.

I have cut a lot of mortices this way
and I used to blunt router cutters with
monotonous regularity. Sharpening was
not a good idea as the amount of money
saved is small and they reduce in size
each time, and this technique requires
consistency of size. The answer
appeared in the form of a KWO
Versofix cutter supplied by Wealden
which has a single replaceable blade –
each blade has two cutting edges and
each cutting edge lasts a good deal
longer than an ordinary TCT cutter –
at least that is my experience so far.

Mitres

Next the mitre must be cut on the rails.
The bottom rail is no problem but the

tip has this fragile cross-grain finger. I
use a disc sander here with an accurately
set platform snug up against the
revolving disc, with only enough space
to allow it to spin.

The mitres are marked with a scalpel
using a mitre gauge. Sand the corner
away until you are just short of the
scribed line and offer it up to the stile to
see if the angle is just so. Correct any
inaccuracies by eye.

Frame assembly

All the rail mitres are cut like this and
the door frame is ready for assembly.
Do a quick dry-assembly to check that
all is well, then apply glue and clamp
up tightly. When making square panels
I usually cut a groove in the stiles and
rails, make and finish the panel, and
assemble the frame around it. In this
case I did not do this because cutting
a groove into the fragile points of the

Cutting curves

I treat the top rail as two pieces, which ensures that the two curves will match exactly and will reduce problems when cutting with the router as each cut will be in the correct direction in relation to the grain of the wood.

The required curve, from side to centre, is designed using either a compass, French Curves, or anything else deemed appropriate.

A litho plate, which is a very thin sheet of aluminium that can be scribed with a sharp steel point, and when flexed, will snap cleanly along the line, can be useful here – you can get them from your local scrap metal merchant. Scribe the chosen shape onto the litho plate with a single clean line and snap off the excess. It is best to support the litho plate as it is flimsy and a little pacing out will assist the routing operation.

The shape is traced onto a piece of scrap hardboard which is then cut on the bandsaw so it is a fraction smaller than the litho plate and will not obstruct the reference edge. The two are joined together with double-sided tape. It is worth noting at this point that once the hardboard is stuck to the litho plate it develops a left-hand/right-hand property. If the routing is to be done on a bench-mounted router, then it should be a right-hand curve, but if a hand-held router is to be used then it should be a left-hand curve.

The litho/hardboard sandwich is then placed on the timber cut for the top rail. Its edge is traced onto the timber which is then flipped over and the operation repeated. The waste is then cut away on the bandsaw about 2mm (⅛in) from the traced line. A top bearing cutter is fitted into a bench-mounted router and the bearing aligned with the litho plate which is fixed to the timber with double-sided tape.

The litho plate will guide the cutter to create the exact curve required. The litho plate and the hardboard are then carefully removed, and re-attached to the reverse side of the timber and the second cut made.

After cutting the top of the panels it is best to move on to cutting the plinth which uses exactly the same techniques.

Detail of curved arch stile

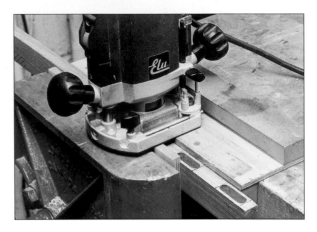

A simple jig to cut the loose tongue mortices

Cutting the mitre on the stile, using a block to guide the chisel

top rail, unsupported by being glued to the stile, could lead to disaster.

When the frame is dry, rebate from the rear 17mm (⅝in) deep and 10mm (⅜in) wide, removing the unsightly tenon.

Panel

The panels are then prepared – they are made up from a single piece of oak, just over half the width of the required panel. It needs to be a nice piece, with clean grain, preferably 32mm (1¼in) thick, but you can get away with 25mm (1in) timber if it is good, flat and a generous measurement. One side is planed flat and the edges squared. It is then re-sawn in half and the surfaces planed and thicknessed to 10mm (⅜in) if possible.

The two pieces are then book-matched and butt-jointed with a little reinforcing from biscuits. Care should be taken not to place a biscuit too close to the ends of the joint as this panel is to be raised and the rebate could cut into the biscuit slot – 'mess up, start again'.

The panel is then sanded flat and offered up to the completed frame, and its outline traced onto it from inside the rebate. It is then cut to size, allowing room for the timber to expand a little at the sides, and taking care in cutting the top curved edge as this edge is the reference edge when the panel is raised.

Raising the panel involves cutting a rebate into the front edge about 30mm (1¼in) wide and 5mm (¼in) deep, using a shaped cutter. I use a spindle moulder fitted with a ring-fence for this, but it

can be done with a bench-mounted router and the appropriate cutter. The panel should be re-finished and oiled, and inserted into the rebate. It is held in place by what are best described as glazing bars. The reason for oiling the panel at this stage is because it will move within the frame and, if it is oiled after assembly, a line of unfinished timber will become visible when the panel contracts.

Electrics

I am no electronics expert but generally speaking equipment such as hi-fi amplifiers like to be kept cool and need air to circulate. With this in mind I avoided using unnecessary panels such as dust panels between drawers, or base panels. The shelves I made for the

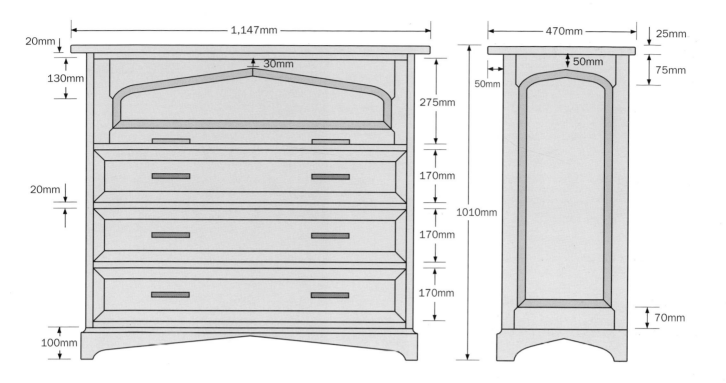

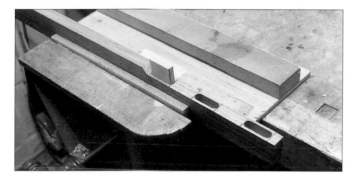

Ply loose tongues act as tenons

A paring chisel is used to clean up the face surface of the mortices

equipment to stand on are drilled with a grid of holes and the back panel is made with a slot at the top to allow hot air to vent. The unit is also made so that, as far as possible, all cables can be contained within it without showing themselves and looking a mess. This meant that I had to allow for various speaker and power cables to drop behind the drawers and remain unseen until they emerged at the base.

Drawers
The drawers were designed with function in mind. They were to contain CDs which would be stored in rows, front to back, with each CD upright showing its spine label. Stored like this, it is necessary that the drawers pull all the way out so that the CDs at the back

can be easily removed. This meant using fully extending sliders, and bearing in mind that each drawer would contain up to 200 CDs, the sliders needed to be strong. Isaac Lord sell the ideal item – not beautiful but very good quality and strong.

The drawers are no more than a box with a ply base with dividers running front to back to keep the CDs in line – the drawer fronts are the pretty bit and they are planted on after the drawer has been installed.

Top
Finally, the top is made. It is solid oak made up from two pieces butt-jointed together, reinforced with biscuits and fitted with standard wooden buttons.

The final finish is oil – for oak I like

Suppliers

Wealden Tool Company
tel: 0800 328 4183
fax: 0700 054636
KWO Tools tel: 01732 364444
Liberon tel: 01797 367555
Isaac Lord tel: 01494 462121

Liberon Finishing Oil as it has less colour than some others and is more suitable for lighter woods. A little wax to complete the job brightens it up and gives it a nice smell. ■

Mike Cowie turned to cabinetmaking after being made redundant. After passing with distinction a City & Guilds course at Sheffield, he set up his own workshop and is now in the happy position of having as much work as he can cope with

PHOTOGRAPHS BY THE AUTHOR

Modern televisions are not the most elegant objects – one option is to hide it all away in something more delicate

Period drama

Mike Cowie makes a classically inspired TV cabinet.
Part 1 – the base

I first met Steve and Janet Oatway while delivering some work to Gallery 13 at Epworth, between Doncaster and Scunthorpe. Steve was quite taken with my work, but Janet was very cool – and still is! I have to add that this is due more to style than workmanship, thankfully, for Janet is disdainful of all but traditional design and nothing I could say would sway her from this.

The irony of it was that the proposed piece of furniture was to house a wide-screen TV, complete with video and satellite receiver – a modern home entertainment system! A requirement was that the top of the TV was to sit 1015mm (40in) from the floor. I do hope Janet will forgive me for mentioning this, but her initial request was for cabriole legs. I imagined a giant unit lumbering under

the weight of the TV and carefully informed Janet of the impracticality of this. Thankfully, concessions were made.

I did some drawings, initially looking for a balanced unit. When happy with the dimensions, I sought a design that would satisfy Janet's wishes. Given the constraints, this was fairly straightforward, so I dispatched drawings, received approval and started work.

I bought the selected timber, American walnut (*Juglans nigra*), from Duffields, near Ripon – I often traipse about with 10 cubic feet or so of timber on the roof rack! Having safely delivered it to the workshop, I cut the wood to approximate lengths and left it to settle for a couple of weeks.

The weight of the TV gave me some concern, for lightweight they certainly are

not! Steve had asked me not to put a back in the lower unit – so it would be easier to install the TV, with its multitude of wires. That left my cabinet without a strong back support – but then problems exist to make life more interesting!

Short-handed clamps

Eventually I could start work and I planed the walnut to size, aiming for 25mm (1in) thickness, but in the end had to settle for 22mm (⅞in). I glued it up with butt joints and left it to set. However, the inevitable shortage of clamps played its part, so I did it in stages – how many clamps are ever enough?

I am a firm believer in removing excess glue while it's still rubbery – otherwise you can end up digging into the wood by

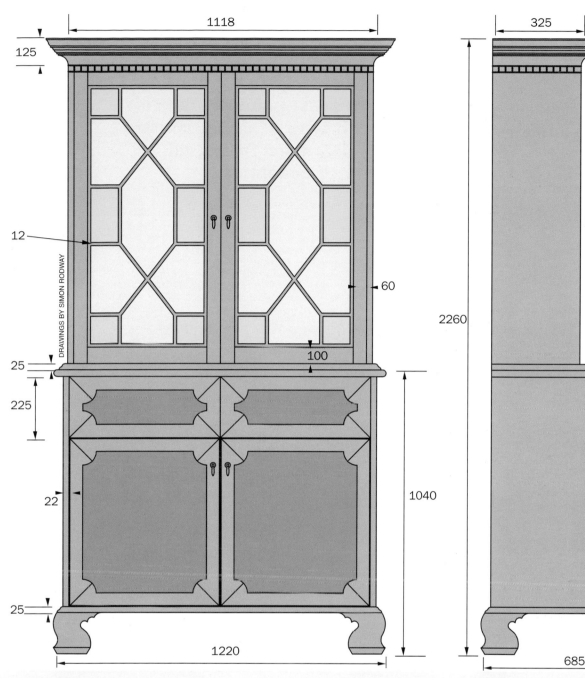

All
measurements
are in
millimetres

DRAWINGS BY SIMON RODWAY

mistake while chipping off hardened glue. When you remove the wood from the clamps the amount of clean-up work needed depends on how much care you took with the preparation. A good job will require only a thin skim with a sharp plane, while a poor job will entail major restructuring work to bring everything level.

Using a combination of plane, scraper and orbital sander I obtained a satisfactory surface. The scraper alone would be my chosen weapon, were it not for its annoying tendency to burn thumbs. I have invested in a wooden holder, but find this wholly impractical, because it numbs the feel of what you're doing almost as badly as if you were wearing plasters on thumbs! Sometimes I put up with this, for occasions when a sharp

scraper at an acute angle is invaluable.

My next task was to select panels for face and edge, aiming for uniformity of grain. This done, I always pass the boards over the planer to get a good working edge and, working from this, mark out the required dimensions. Next I cut it to size with a Festo portable saw and guide rail system. The drawback to this is that the edges need dressing with a sharp plane to remove the blade marks. Both sides are planed together so that any inaccuracies will be matched and unnoticeable. The chosen construction was dovetails for strength on the bottom and tenons on the top. Well-fitting dovetails always bring a smile of satisfaction – and relief – regarded as the epitome of craftsmanship, yet I warrant each maker will have a slightly different

method of cutting. My favourite tool is the bandsaw, with a Japanese Ikedane saw as back-up – two very different tools, giving an almost identical result. I find dovetail saws dangerous – the scars on my thumb are positive proof – it couldn't possibly be my carelessness, could it!

Cutting line

I set the marking gauge to score a cutting line – I have recently been asked, twice, what these lines are for and my explanation that they are the product of handmade work met with bemusement. I believe they are a necessary evil for to plane them off would add a considerable element to the job.

I cut the dovetails and did a trial fit. I put them to one side and marked the underside of the top to receive mortices

Secret swivel

An added complication was that the TV needed to swivel slightly. With the type of doors chosen this meant fitting an inner assembly. I'd also suggested a slide-out tray for the video. This meant more planing and gluing up. It had to be strong so I elected for through-tenon construction, cut with the router. Space was tight and it would be a shoehorn job to get all the appliances in. Roller-bearing runners were used for the slide, with a slip of walnut on the front to conceal them. As for the swivel, I went for the largest I could obtain – 300mm (almost 12in). To save 5mm (³⁄₁₆in) of space, I routed out a recess so that the bearing might fit in this. As an added benefit – obviously due to my foresight – when placing the TV, the bearing stayed in place. I screwed to the upper leaf through cutouts done for this purpose. The whole assembly was then screwed in place from the underside, a little tricky but eventually managed.

Mike used a larger version of this type of swivel

Pocket doors

Pocket doors were relatively new to me. For the uninitiated, they allow the door to open normally then slide into the cabinet on a rail system – very handy for TV cabinets! I wanted to give the impression of a normal door with drawer above. It is actually one piece, the base being 18mm (³⁄₄in) MDF with a burr walnut veneer.

Pocket doors are more convenient in this situation, when space is tight and you want doors open for hours at a time

❝An added complication was that the TV needed to swivel slightly. With the type of doors chosen this meant fitting an inner assembly❞

Balancing veneer

MDF

Burr veneer

Solid carcass

The feet needed to be strong but decorative

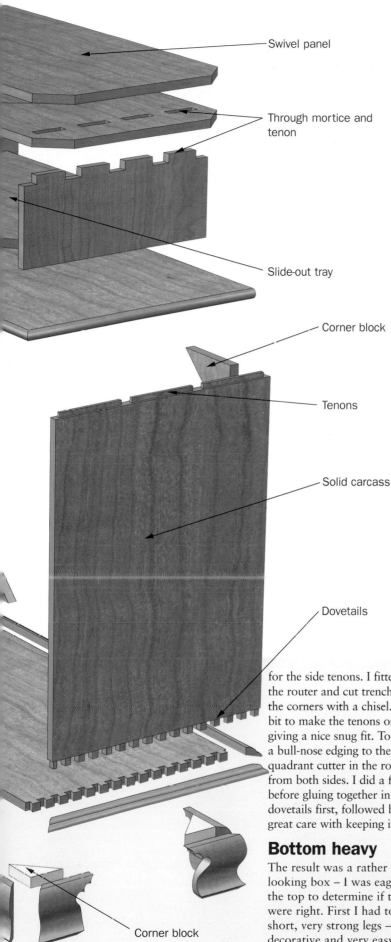

Swivel panel

Through mortice and tenon

Slide-out tray

Corner block

Tenons

Solid carcass

Dovetails

Corner block

In a vacuum

I had for some time been considering purchasing a vacuum-bag press to better utilise the versatility of veneering. This job gave me an incentive to put my hand in my pocket and obtain a professional kit. The only complaint I have is the lack of information on usage!

Sourcing veneer in small quantities proved slightly difficult – and expensive. However, Scottish Veneers of Leeds came to my aid with a nice piece of book-matched burr walnut at a fair price – from their warehouse full of veneers. Due to the price and the fact that one error could ruin all, I made a template out of MDF before cutting the veneer, adding cross-banding to the edges. It was all held in place by Sellotape. I used Extramite for gluing and did one door at a time, though the bag can hold much more. For the first time I was taking great care.

What a pleasure to see the efficiency – the air quickly vacated and the veneer didn't move – resulting in a really excellent job, so I've now burnt my cauls! Ah, but that was the easy part – the inlay was a mite trickier, especially cutting grooves for the inlay.

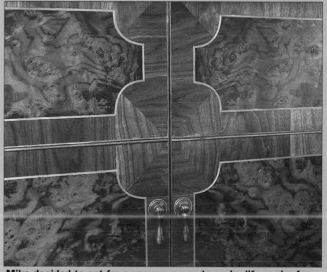

Mike decided to opt for a vacuum press to make life easier for the detailed veneering he was undertaking

for the side tenons. I fitted a 12mm bit in the router and cut trenches, squaring up the corners with a chisel. I used a 19mm bit to make the tenons on the side panels, giving a nice snug fit. To finish, I applied a bull-nose edging to the top, using a quadrant cutter in the router and working from both sides. I did a final clean-up before gluing together in two stages – dovetails first, followed by the top, taking great care with keeping it square.

Bottom heavy

The result was a rather large, heavy-looking box – I was eager to get on with the top to determine if the proportions were right. First I had to make some short, very strong legs – nicely decorative and very easy to make. Taking a length of walnut long enough

for eight sides and possibly one spare, I made a template and marked the position of each leg roughly.

I used a 35mm Forstner bit to drill a hole through to create the tight arch, then I used a 20mm cove cutter in the router to make a series of cuts along the length to form the concave shape of the leg. I then faired it in with a swan-neck scraper. Angling the table saw to 15°, I made a bevel for the lower edge and a 45° bevel for the top edge to remove excess material. I used a block plane, scraper and sandpaper to create a pleasant, undulating curve. Using the Forstner hole as a guide, I laid the template back on and pencilled in the shape. Bear in mind that these are right- and left-handed templates, though, or a moment's carelessness could give eight

Swivelling shelf on top of the TV support

Close-up of the pocket door mechanism

‘**Power tools can ruin work much faster than handwork, particularly the router if you don't watch out!**’

Useful addresses

Vacuum veneering:
The Air Press Company, 01725 514429 for a dedicated system.

Isaac Lord Ltd, Unit 5, Hawkfield Close, Hawkfield Business Park, Whitchurch, Bristol BS14 OBL. Tel: 0117 978 8900. Fax: 0117 935 9898.

Scottish Veneers of Leeds, PO Box 528, York YO24 2YH. Tel: 01904 778704. Fax: 01904 778705. Furniture-makers welcome to visit London warehouse.

Further reading

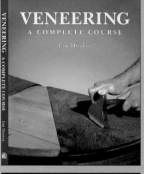

Veneering – A Complete Course, by Ian Hosker, GMC, £16.95, colour pb, ISBN 1 86108 046 8.

The Veneering Book by David Shath Square, Taunton, £16.95, colour pb, ISBN 1 56158 093 7.

Both books are available by mail order from GMC Publications Ltd, tel: 01273 488005.

right-hand parts!

Now I could cut the mitres and for this I adapted a sledge, running in the mitre slots on the table saw. I cut the inner mitres on the bandsaw with a 5mm blade and cleaned up with a rasp and files. I needed to retouch the mitres with a plane for a good fit, then I glued and Sellotaped the pairs together to set. I used the orbital sander to clean up the legs, with a quick touch-up with a plane on the bevel, then added a strong fillet behind. I added a corner brace with two screw holes for attaching to the body. Prior to fitting the legs I needed to create a moulding along the bottom. For this I cut a rebate with the router, so that the moulding didn't look stuck on.

Now I screwed the legs in position and it started to look better. As there would be no back, I decided to add some corner braces for rigidity.

Power fears

Power tools can ruin work much faster than handwork, particularly the router if you don't watch out! Straight lines are straightforward, but quadrants are a problem. I adapted the veneer template, fitted a guide bush to the router and with careful measuring clamped it to the door. Having done some trial cuts, I placed stops on the template and apprehensively cut the first one. Confidence built up as I completed all successfully – however, I said to myself 'be careful, this is going too well'.

The inlay was alder (*alnus glutinosa*), chosen as much for the colour as its bending ability. I cut it into strips for the quadrants, boiled them in a pan of water, steamed and bent them over a former – and left them to dry.

A little bit of work with a sanding block gave a good fit. I glued the quadrants in place and left the straight lines till last, making it easier to mitre the corners. Once all the inlay was glued in I carefully planed it flush and sanded it. To give the effect of a door with a drawer, I routed out a groove and shaped a strip of walnut to resemble pieces of cockbeading shaped with a scratchstock. After cleaning up the doors, checking for fit, a cockbeading was glued around the edges, protecting the veneer.

Fitting of the doors is not as precise as for normal hinges – I used a kitchen cabinet hinge with built-in adjustment. I tried it out with a piece of scrap first, because the instructions left a little to be desired. I drilled 35mm holes in the doors, fixed the assembly in place and adjusted the doors. Although not necessary, I fitted brass ball-catches with a wooden stop on the bottom, which I found more satisfying. ■

Mike Cowie turned to cabinetmaking after being made redundant. After passing with distinction a City & Guilds course at Sheffield, he set up his own workshop and is now in the happy position of having as much work as he can cope with

Modern televisions are not the most elegant – one option is to hide it all away in something more delicate

PHOTOGRAPHS BY STEPHEN HEPWORTH

Period drama
Part 2

Mike Cowie completes his classically inspired TV cabinet. Part 2 – the upper case

In the previous article I explained how I made the bottom unit, which was quite large. I was anxious to get on with the top, to ensure the proportion was right for the sides, and had saved two lovely wide book-matched boards of walnut from a previous batch. I made up the top and bottom from narrower stock, dovetail construction all round for strength, chopped out and tested for fit. I cut a rebate on the sides for the back panel with the router and cut in the hinges prior to gluing together. Jigs are available for fitting hinges; however, if a router is available I think there is no better method. Simply mark the position

of the hinges, numbered for accuracy, square up the side lines with a marking knife, scribe in the width and adjust the router to this line. Set the depth and for the first cut, a back or climb cut to take a nibble off the front – this avoids breakout. Then plunge in to the back and remove the waste. Finally, square the edges with a chisel. It is beneficial of course if the doors can be done at the same time; however, this is rarely possible though the router can be set from one of the completed cuts. Five minutes to complete all six hinges and yet I still see advice on how to chop hinges with a chisel!

Another little job before gluing is to cut the recess for the library strip. You can buy a special cutter for this, however a 19mm bit in the router followed by a 10mm bit to form a stepped cut suffices.

The frame can now be glued together and care with the diagonals always saves problems later. This is usually a fraught time, but it never ceases to amaze me that out of this untidy mess emerges a handsome cabinet – usually!

I routed a rebate around both top and bottom of the unit – for a moulding to sit on the bottom and the cornice at the top. On the bench, I cut holes for downlighters freehand with the router.

Painful panes

I normally like to get on with a job, enjoying the flow of work. Glazing bars, however, test the patience, although they do add to the variety of work.

Plane down some walnut to 12mm (½in), then carefully pass it over the spindle moulder fitted with an 8mm half-round cutter then cut off at the table saw. The strip is repeatedly passed over the planer until sufficient bars are produced.

That satisfies the front face – the back, however, requires a 3mm (⅛in) groove running up the centre. For this I found the easiest way was to rout out a groove in a thick piece of ash to nestle the glazing bars in, with stops at either end. From there, it is a simple matter to plane the back level and set the router fence to plunge a 3mm (⅛in) groove along the length.

With this complete, knowing the size of the glazing bars, you can make a template. Made from a length of plywood, this simply fits into the recess on the back of the door. Draw the required position of the glazing bars onto it.

Using this, mark off with a sharp knife the position of the bars on the edges of the door and using the mitre block, nibble out a slight 'V' with a sharp chisel. I first made a slight saw-cut down the middle, as this made things much easier. When all mitres were complete around the door, I placed the template back in, remaining there until complete – it helps enormously to wax the template first! Gradually cut and place the bars to conform with the template, tacks hammered into place assist with this. Bisecting the angles on the template gives the required angle to cut to; aim for a nice tight fit with no play. With all bars cut and fitted to satisfaction, remove and glue in place before setting aside to harden.

To achieve the mitres I used a mix of Japanese saw, mitre guillotine and chisels – whatever suits. When set, the doors require 3mm (⅛in) strips gluing into the slots very carefully. Once planed up and finished by hand to achieve a good fit, they were butt-jointed at the edges and carefully glued in place. This can be assisted by laying the whole door on a supporting panel, where pressure can safely be applied. Cloth is then glued across each joint to give additional strength and help to make the joints surprisingly strong – which is just as well, really! Danish oil should be applied as the work progresses – particularly on the glazing bars before the glass is fitted.

Above **Interior fittings**

Below **Challenging mitres and purple cathedral glass**

Cut-glass accidents

Now to the tricky bit – glazing. Any glaziers will no doubt laugh at this. However, I am no glazier and for my sins had suggested a rippled glass for effect. The problem was that I had obtained two matching pieces of glass with a slight curve to the pattern and if one was spoilt then so was the other. So it was with some trepidation that I approached cutting the glass and the best advice I can give is – be bold! Glass is, I believe, always cut on the flat side, so take care to ensure the pattern follows correctly. To my great amazement and delight it was a success – I actually began to enjoy the process.

For a bit of colour, I included some purple cathedral glass in the smaller square/rectangular sections. In my anxiety to see the effect of this glass I managed to turn the door over with some pieces in place – not a good idea on a concrete floor! Fortunately I was able to replace the broken piece. The best part is puttying up – a task akin to plastering – best left alone.

Putty it had to be, though. The first problem proved to be obtaining brown putty which, curiously, my glass supplier did not stock. I eventually obtained some, only to find it was so runny it was unusable. The second lot of putty I bought proved to be just as bad and I was forced to resort to placing bits of putty on cardboard to allow it to dry out enough to be used. I used a putty knife and a great deal of care, and – as with glass – it proved best to be firm and I just began to get the hang of it as the job was finished.

I wiped off the excess smears of putty on the glass and walnut as soon as possible, then left the doors in a warm room so the putty could set.

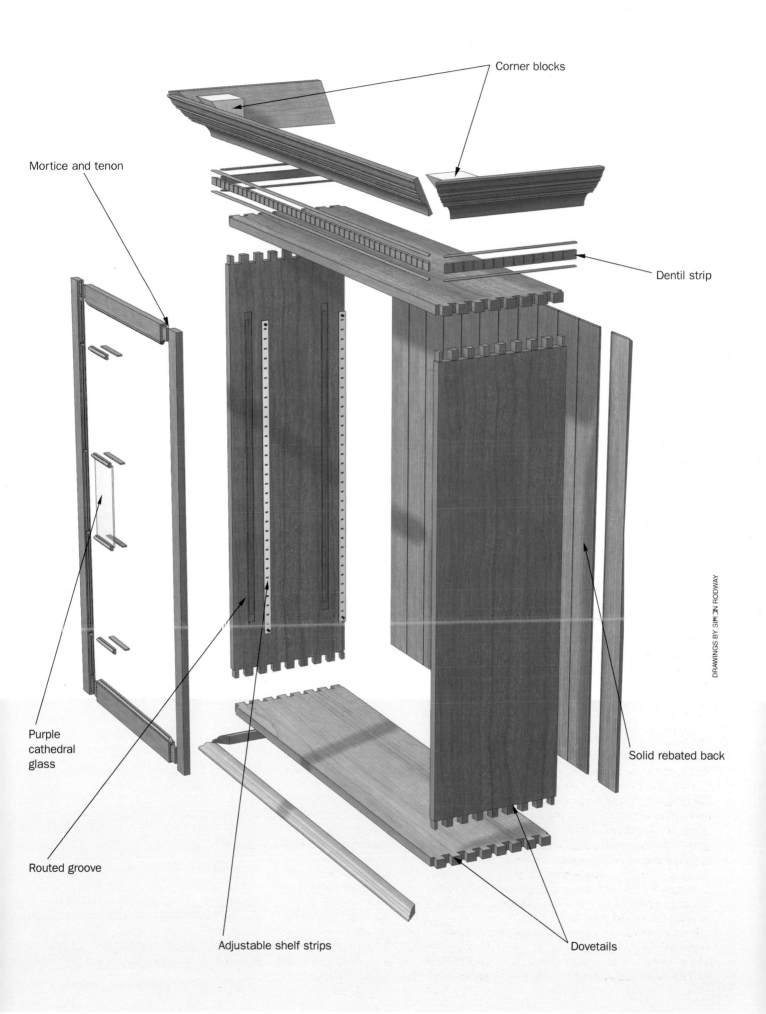

Corner blocks

Mortice and tenon

Dentil strip

Purple
cathedral
glass

Solid rebated back

Routed groove

Adjustable shelf strips

Dovetails

DRAWINGS BY SIMON RODWAY

'My solid walnut
for the back
panel, sadly, had
to be thicknessed
down to 10mm
(⅜in) from 25mm
(1in) stock'

Wasted walnut

My solid walnut for the back panel, sadly, had to be thicknessed down to 10mm (⅜in) from 25mm (1in) stock. What a waste! I cut a rebate on alternative edges of these panels to half the depth – 5mm (¼in) so that they may be butted together allowing a 2mm (⁵⁄₆₄in) gap between each. This caused a nice shadow line, also a degree of movement.

The best part I have saved until near the end – the doors. Anyone who has tackled this type of door will, I think, agree they are slow and tedious to make at best!

The door frames are made using normal mortice and tenon construction – with the router of course, a 4mm

quadrant cutter on the spindle moulder to form a bead on the face side with a rebate for the glass on the back. The bead was mitred at the corners with a small 45° block clamped onto the frame and held in the vice.

The frames can be glued up now and when set, fitted into the case and hinges cut, then onto the glazing bars

A strip of dentil moulding, cut on the table saw, and a range of mouldings, cut on the spindle moulder, served to produce the cornice, built up with glue blocks behind to secure it.

I applied Danish oil for the finish. I left it to dry and rubbed it down with a grey Webrax pad, applying roughly six coats on a daily basis until delivery. ∎

Completed top – glazed and polished

An inspired piece

PHOTOGRAPHY BY
THE AUTHOR
ILLUSTRATIONS BY
SIMON RODWAY

Andrew Lawton

makes a clothes chest
with an Arts & Crafts
influence

**Views of
the chest**

Andrew Lawton, a member of the Society of Designer
Craftsmen, has been making furniture full time since 1980. His
workshop in Derbyshire was once owned by pioneer craftsman
Ben Coopland and was saved from dereliction by Andrew.
He has recently received a second Guild Mark, in conjunction
with Young Jones, for a millennium cabinet

This clothes chest was the last piece in a series of related cabinets which were commissioned for the master bedroom of a recently built house. The other pieces consisted of a tall chest of eight drawers, a low chest of three drawers, and a larger cabinet to the same design as this one. They are replacements for factory-made pine pieces which had been passed on to the client's children who were setting up homes. This must be quite a common occurrence for many makers – clients who decide to upgrade the cheap and cheerful furniture of earlier years by commissioning high-quality bespoke work.

Design

The design of this cabinet was directly inspired by an early Edward Barnsley cupboard of oak, made in 1919. The original cupboard is very much in the no-nonsense Arts & Crafts style with its dovetailed carcass, bold door components and gently arched plinth rail.

My clients have a preference for lighter coloured timbers, hence the choice of white ash for their bedroom project. The character of the ash and the understated design were intended to complement the decor of the room and help give an atmosphere of serenity and restfulness.

Timber

The timber, already kiln-dried when bought, had been in stock for some time, kept on a platform in the roofspace of the workshop, so could be confidently used without the normal precaution of roughing out all the various parts and allowing them to settle down. The main potential problem, as far as movement was concerned, was the door panels, which had to be deep-sawn from 25mm (1in) thick boards to yield panels of an eventual finished thickness of not less than 9mm (⅜in). To have planed them

down to this thickness would obviously have been very wasteful, so the boards were ripped down through their thickness on the bandsaw.

Unless you are fortunate enough to be able to have a log sawn to your own specification there isn't much that can be done about this, since most timber merchants don't stock timber less than 25mm in thickness, apart from oak and sweet chestnut intended specifically for drawer sides. Luckily, after a week or so the deeped boards had only cupped very slightly and after machining to their intended finished dimensions, stayed flat and true. The closer the timber can remain to being quarter-sawn will increase the chances of the boards remaining flat after deep-sawing – flat-sawn or tangentially-sawn oak is one of the worst offenders in this respect.

Construction

Start construction with the top, bottom, sides and central division of the carcass. Each of these components is of two

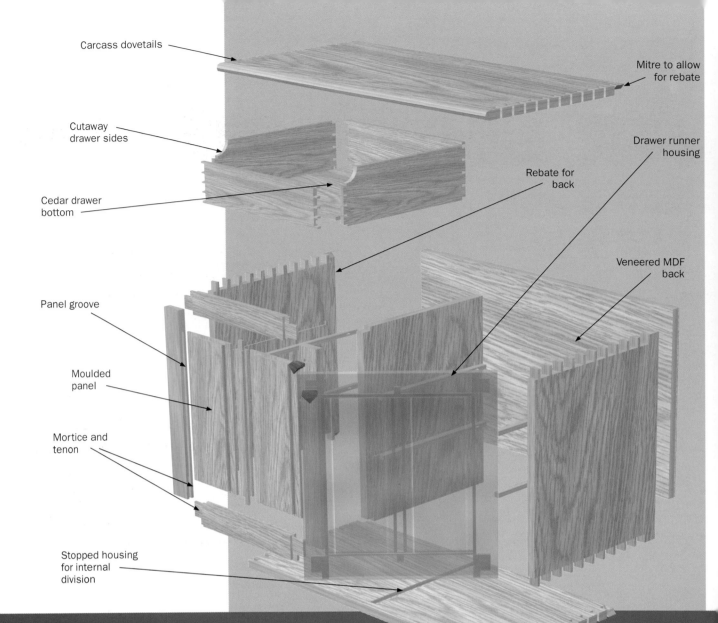

Carcass dovetails

Cutaway
drawer sides

Cedar drawer
bottom

Panel groove

Moulded
panel

Mortice and
tenon

Stopped housing
for internal
division

Mitre to allow
for rebate

Drawer runner
housing

Rebate for
back

Veneered MDF
back

Stub tenons

Buttons located
in groove

boards jointed at the middle – try to find
a good grain match especially for the top.
After carefully truing and squaring up,
mark out all the various shoulder lines
and housings with a knife. Time spent at
the marking-out stage is always amply
repaid when it comes to gluing up the
carcass and fitting the drawers and
doors. Incidentally, my marking knife is
nothing more elaborate than an old
mechanical hacksaw blade suitably
ground and made user-friendly with
sticky tape.

As usual, the dovetails are left until
after the housings have been cut to
prevent the vulnerable disassembled
joints from accidental damage,
particularly the mitres at the back, which
the back is later fitted into.

Housings

The housings are cut using a 9mm
tungsten-tipped cutter in the trusty Elu
96E router, using an engineer's straight-
edge cramped to the workpiece to act as
a fence. The main vertical division is

eased into its housings until a tight hand
fit is achieved. The dovetails are
subsequently cut by hand, marking the
pins from the tails in conventional
fashion, with the aforementioned mitres
at the back of the carcass, allowing the
rebates to be run right through on all
four components. The division is
narrower than the other parts by the
width of the rebates, with the back panel
butting tight up to it.

The internal faces are then sanded – all
parts which will later be glued, blanked

off with masking tape, and the whole of
the interior waxed and polished off. The
advantages of doing this are that any
squeezed out glue can easily be lifted off
with a sharp chisel after it has set, since it
doesn't stick to the wax – plus it is much
easier to do a thorough job before
assembly when there are no awkward
internal corners to deal with. Also,
despite our best efforts at preparing the
timber, marking out and so on,
sometimes the internal faces of a carcass
will need truing up after it has been put

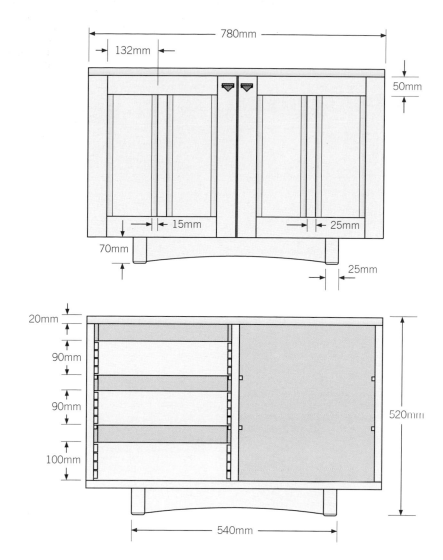

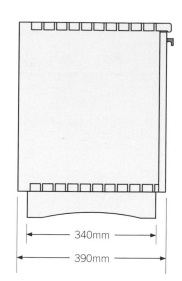

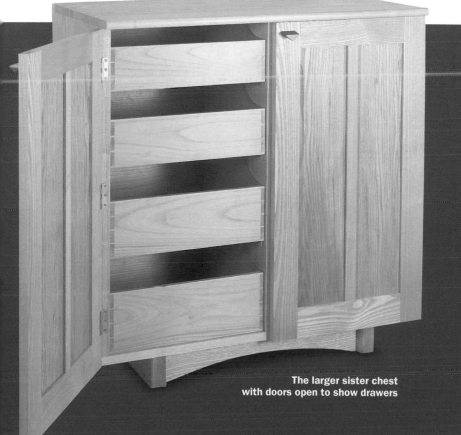

'The character of the ash and the understated design were intended to complement the decor of the room and help give an atmosphere of serenity and restfulness'

The larger sister chest with doors open to show drawers

together, if it is to be fitted with drawers. Waxed surfaces in conjunction with a straight edge and plane can be useful in showing where shavings have been removed.

Gluing up

David Charlesworth offers sound advice when he advises cabinetmakers to break down the gluing-up stage into a series of carefully planned operations.

To begin with, the central division is glued to the base to form an inverted 'T', rather than attempting the whole glue-up in one go. It is important not to introduce any sort of bowing, convex or concave, when gluing partitions or shelves into a carcass, but it can happen all too easily if a component is a shade too short to reach the full depth of its housing, or a stray bit of debris has become lodged unnoticed in the housing. It is always a good idea to have a clean-up of the working area, not forgetting your own clothing, to get rid of those rogue router chippings and bits of

Learning from the past

On a historical note, Stanley Davies of Windermere often used this form of panel – adding an inventive touch to traditionally built solid wood furniture. On my piece the aim was to disguise the near-squareness of the doors by breaking them up into smaller rectangles and stressing the verticals.

Chaucer cabinet in English walnut by Alan Peters – made to house the William Morris Kelmscott Press edition of Chaucer's works

ABOVE **Tall chest of drawers in same room scheme**

BELOW **Inside of carcass base showing dovetails and mitred rebate to take back**

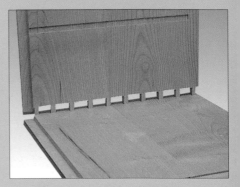

ABOVE **Carcass joints offered up to check fit of dovetails**

sawdust. The best way to ensure that everything is pulled up flat and true is to have a selection of purpose-made, stout bearers, some with a slightly convex edge on one side, to give an even distribution of cramping pressure.

The next day the assembly of the carcass is completed by adding the sides and the top. A pair of sash cramps and bearers are again used to pull the division into its housing, but the dovetails are driven down with a hammer and flat block, just as one would assemble a drawer. Cramps are used to finally pull the shoulders tight and ensure that the mitres are closed up, and are left on overnight.

Plinth

As a respite from the carcass, the plinth is made next. This is just a simple frame, jointed with double stub tenons. The curves on the front and back rails are worked first on the bandsaw followed by a spokeshave and light sanding. The feet are slightly recessed in the middle to ensure that the cabinet will sit firmly on the floor without any tendency to rock. As the grain of the feet is at right angles to the carcass base, the plinth is attached with buttons to accommodate any movement across the grain. At this stage, the outside is given a final clean-up with a sharp smoothing plane and scraper plane.

Doors

The doors are of straightforward haunched mortice and tenon construction, grooved to take the panels, which take advantage of the fact that for all practical purposes timber doesn't shrink or swell in its length. Thus they are rebated to fit tightly into the top and bottom rails with a cove moulding worked on the vertical edges only.

Mortices

The mortices are chopped on a hollow chisel morticer while the tenons and grooves are done on a table saw; alternatively this can all be achieved with a router, or entirely by hand, if you prefer! The rebates and coving of the panels are carried out with the router and suitable cutters, mounted in a shop-made table which clamps securely in the jaws of the vice on one side and is propped up on the other side by a hinged leg – when not in use it simply folds up and hangs on the wall.

Care must be taken to ensure that the sash cramps are absolutely level when gluing up the doors so that no twisting or 'winding' is introduced. Solid wood panels must never be glued all round into the grooves, of course, but a dab of glue ought to be applied to the middle 25mm (1in) or so top and bottom so they are not completely loose.

Fitting

After cleaning up, the doors are shot to fit the carcass and hung on good-quality solid drawn brass butt hinges. At this moment the positions of the mortice for

'As the grain of the feet is at right angles to the carcass base, the plinth is attached with buttons to accommodate any movement across the grain'

Carcass and plinth ready for joining together with buttons

Routing door panels on shop-made router table

Underside of drawer showing cedar bottom slot-screwed in-place

Constructional details of door showing panel rebates and moulding

the door pulls are established, and they are then cut with the router. I came up with the design of this knob a few years ago and haven't been able to better it yet; consequently it gets used on a lot of my work – a kind of trademark almost.

Using a dark wood – American walnut in this case – provides a visual contrast and, from a practical angle, will not become discoloured from the accumulation of oil from peoples' fingers over the years.

The doors, at this stage hung with one screw in each hinge only, are removed and the inside of the carcass checked over with a straight edge, any high spots removed and re-waxed, as described earlier. The runners are hand-planed to be a snug fit in their housings, glued for the first 50mm (2in) or so and slot-screwed at the back. If the housings are accurately cut in the first place, then the runners will be parallel too. These drawers could easily have been side-hung, but the space between each is there for a good reason – to prevent fluffy jumpers and other items of clothing from catching on the bottoms of the drawer above — a tip from Ernest Joyce's *Technique of Furniture Making*.

The drawer fronts are cut away to show the contents and to make opening them easier in the absence of applied handles.

Materials

Oak was used for the sides and fronts, partly to add an extra dimension, instead of employing ash throughout, but also with the possible problems of distortion associated with deep-sawing the ash very much in mind. Cedar of Lebanon was a natural, but by no means essential, choice for the bottoms. I saw an attractive and finely made chest of drawers in an exhibition a couple of years ago with re-dyed 6mm (¼in) thick MDF drawer bottoms, and most effective it was too.

The actual making of the drawers has been well enough documented not to need repeating; all I will add is that through, rather than lapped, dovetails are used to give a decorative effect to the drawer fronts when both the doors are open.

Assembly

Once the drawers are fitting to your satisfaction, the pre-veneered MDF carcass back is glued into place. It is often a good idea to screw the cabinet back in place, to make removal an easy matter, if for any reason it has to come off – but on a small, relatively simple piece such as this, with all internal parts easily accessible, gluing is fine.

Finishing

Finally, the recessed magnetic catches are fitted, the chest sanded down to 320 grit, and sprayed with pre-catalysed matt lacquer, which is de-nibbed and buffed up with a soft cloth after allowing it to fully cure for a few days. ■

Keeper of secrets

PHOTOGRAPHY BY ANTHONY BAILEY
ILLUSTRATIONS BY SIMON RODWAY
AND IAN HALL

Having returned to the UK after a number of years abroad, Duncan Lyall enrolled on a City & Guilds furniture design course at Kendal College, before acquiring workshop space to produce both batch production and commissioned work

Subtle curves help alleviate the squareness usually found on modern chests of drawers

Eight months into the first year of my City and Guilds course at Kendal College, and with all digits intact, I was finally given free rein to produce my first design-and-make project.

Commissions being a bit thin on the ground, I wanted to make something for myself that was practical and, being short of storage space, decided on a three-drawer chest – a project that would incorporate all my recently acquired skills.

Having been impressed by the design philosophy of the Arts and Crafts movement, I hoped to produce an honest piece of simple line, while incorporating a few ideas of my own.

Timber

The design dictated the use of traditional home-grown timber – quarter-sawn English oak (*Quercus robur*) being the obvious choice for the framing, while sycamore (*Acer pseudoplatanus*) gave a pleasant contrast to the drawer sides, backs and base for the compartment under the lid. These two woods lie happily together and, if chosen carefully, the figuring on the sycamore adds interest to the drawer sides. Luckily both these woods were available locally.

As the chest was to be used for clothes storage the aromatic quality of cedar of Lebanon (*Cedrela libani*) seemed the logical choice for the drawer bases. It is still a delight to smell when the drawers are opened.

Skeleton frame

The framework is of straightforward mortice and tenon construction. As I had recently invested in a router I was determined to make maximum use of this versatile tool.

The mortices for the posts are marked out in matching pairs, front and back. With one pair clamped to the bench, the router is fitted with two fences, one against each side of the work. These are then adjusted so that the router slides smoothly along the two posts, cutting the four mortices needed on each face. This works well, leaving only the rounded ends to be cut by hand using a router set in a table – cutting the tenons is equally painless. An offcut, the same thickness as the rails, is used to set the cutter height until a good fitting tenon is produced. Each set of side, back and front rails is then cut exactly to length –

Inner lid up showing the dressing mirror and top compartment

'When drawing up the plans I became aware of a 'dead' space behind the top front rail so I took the opportunity to incorporate two "secret" drawers'

Design

Inspiration for a design may come from the most unusual of sources. In this case it came from an old treadle sewing machine that I have in my home – the skeleton framing for the chest's drawer construction and folding top owe much to the old treadle.

This skeleton frame appealed to me – as well as being reasonably economical with timber it would minimise any movement that might later occur. The exposed drawer sides also gave me the opportunity to use contrasting timbers to highlight the design.

As part of my earlier coursework I had made a small table with legs that curved gently inwards from base to top while retaining a straight inner edge. This seemed to work well, giving an appearance of stability – so that feature was incorporated into this design. Gentle curves were added to the side, back and front rails to continue the theme.

When drawing up the plans I became aware of a 'dead' space behind the top front rail so I took the opportunity to incorporate two 'secret' drawers.

Waney-edged timber

After leaving the wood for a couple of weeks to acclimatise to the conditions in the workshop, the waney-edged boards are planed on one side. Rods are then used to make best use of the figuring available. This was my first experience of waney-edged timber and I was shocked at the wastage once defects were removed – definitely a case of buyer beware – and necessitated another trip to the sawmill. Finally, after the most economical use of the timber had been achieved, it was thicknessed and cut to size.

and in turn laid side by side with a piece of scrap inserted after the last rail to cope with any breakout that may occur. The rails are then clamped together and machined as a unit, so producing accurate work with virtually no need for marking out.

Next job is to cut the stopped housings in the front and back top rails and the corresponding tenons on the three cross-members that together form the sides and divider of the compartment under the hinged top. Rebates are cut into the bottom of these rails later to accept a piece of veneered plywood to form the base of the compartment.

As these rails will be used to attach the top, it is as well to drill and counter-sink them now, especially if a vertical drill stand is available.

The framework is now loosely assembled and checked to ensure that all is square. After disassembly, the posts

and rails are bandsawn to shape. The easiest method I have found to produce these long lazy curves is to use a metre steel rule which can be flexed until the desired curve is achieved. This line can then be easily transferred from rod to workpiece. Cleaning up the curves is done with a circular plane – a tool I find a pleasure to use especially after the incessant whine of the router.

Next rebate the tops of the side-rails – a purely decorative feature which also appears to slim down their width. Finally make the two 'ends' of the front top rail which are then tenoned into the posts.

Assembly

Everything is sanded prior to gluing-up. The nature of the construction means that all work is visible and time spent now is well spent.

Cramping up is straightforward – post and side-rails first. When dry, the two

Economical on wood, the drawer sides are a quiet contrast to the oak frame

TOP
The top consists of a surround and a hinged inner lid. The surround is mitred and biscuited from a single board to ensure continuity of the grain. Matched boards are biscuited together to form the inner lid. 3mm (⅛in) ebony stringing is added around the sides and front.

TOP COMPARTMENT
The three cross members that form the sides and divider of the top compartment are put together using housings and tenons. Rebates are cut into the bottom of these rails to take the veneered ply that forms the bottom of the compartment. They are drilled and counter-sunk to take the top.

FRAMEWORK

The carcass framework is of mortice and tenon construction. The mortices for the legs are marked out in matching pairs, front and back. They are cut with a router using two fences, one against each side of the work. The rounded ends of each mortice then need to be cut by hand. An offcut from the rails can be used to set the cutter height on the router to produce a well-fitting tenon. Each set of side, back, and front rails are then cut exactly to length and each set is laid out with a scrap piece beyond the last rail to avoid any breakout. The rails are then clamped together and machined as a set.

SECRET DRAWERS

The two secret drawers are again dovetailed. Short hardwood pegs are fitted into the base of the back to enable them to be opened from underneath the first drawer. The bottom is a sycamore veneered ply.

DRAWERS

The fronts of the drawers are made of oak and the sides of sycamore, traditionally dovetailed together. The sides have an additional lipping to avoid wear problems. The bottoms are cedar of Lebanon let into all four sides. Ebony stringing is again used to liven up the plain oak fronts.

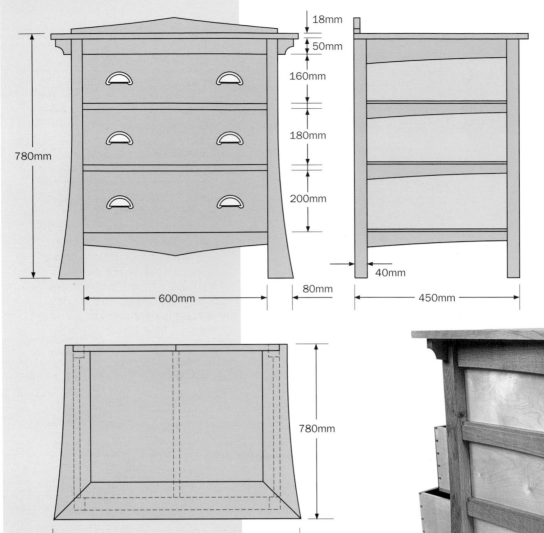

18mm
50mm
160mm
180mm
200mm

780mm

600mm
80mm
40mm
450mm

780mm

800mm

'As these rails will be used to attach the top, it is as well to drill and countersink them now, especially if a vertical drill stand is available'

Back and side with drawers part way out

completed sides and front and rear rails are assembled, ensuring that everything is square. The three cross-rails for the top compartment are then glued in. To complete the job the drawer runners are fitted. The lengths are measured from the assembled framework and then glued and cramped to the side-rails.

Top

The top consists of a surround and hinged inner lid. The surround is made from a single board to ensure a continuity of grain around the sides and front. This is mitred and biscuited

together. Three matching boards are selected to make the hinged lid – these are also biscuited together ensuring that the grain is reversed to minimise any movement that may later occur.

At this point I placed the completed top on the framework to see how things were shaping up. I had originally designed the top rectangular, but now realised that its square edges were out of keeping with the curves of the framework. Shaping the sides inwards from front to back seemed to do the

trick with the added bonus of removing an unsightly knot that had appeared while thicknessing. To complete the top the only remaining job is the addition of 3mm (⅛in) ebony stringing around the sides and front.

Drawers

The drawer casings are made from sycamore and the fronts from oak, dovetailed back and front. The only break from tradition is the addition of a 10mm (⅜in) lipping to the bottom of the drawer sides which will overcome any wear problems that may occur between the soft sycamore sides and oak runners.

'Having been impressed by the design philosophy of the Arts and Crafts movement, I hoped to produce an honest piece of simple line, while incorporating a few ideas of my own'

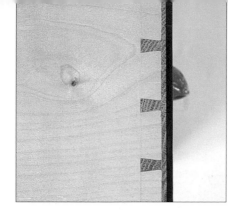

The back

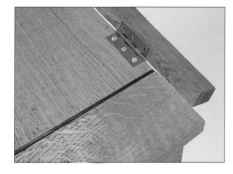

Ebony stringing, traditionally known as cockbeading, around the drawer fronts

Detail showing the top compartment fittings

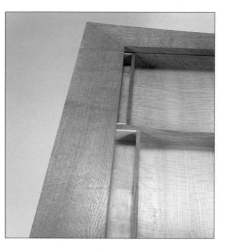

The secret drawers fit neatly between the front rail and the underneath surround of the top

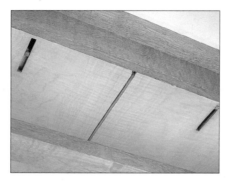

Detail of underneath top compartment showing peg handles for secret drawer

Fittings

Brass fittings and screws are used throughout the construction. I feel these fittings often appear somewhat out of place on handmade furniture. As I have access to a sand/beadblaster all brassware was given the treatment – this softens the colour, and the warm bronze effect complements the colour of the oak.

A particular bugbear of mine are handles that loosen or break in use so I took care when choosing them to ensure that as well as being aesthetically pleasing they were of sturdy design. The ones I chose should prove to be indestructible in use!

Groove for bottom

Veneered ply

Lapped dovetails

Hardwood peg for handle

Through dovetails

The solid cedar of Lebanon drawer bases are made from narrow boards rub-jointed together to the required width. As the backs of the drawers are visible, the bases are let into all four sides. Ebony stringing, as fitted to the top, is also added to the drawer fronts as a contrast to the plain oak.

The two secret drawers are of similar construction and fit behind the top front rail underneath the top surround. To enable the drawers to be opened, short pegs, a fraction longer than the plywood to be used for the compartment bases, are fitted in holes drilled midway along the base of the drawer backs. Sycamore-veneered ply is then cut to size and temporarily fitted in the rebates of the three cross-members and front and back rails to form the compartment base. The positions of the protruding drawer pegs are then marked and slots cut into the ply to allow the drawers to be opened from underneath.

Finish

As all parts of the chest have been sanded prior to assembly finishing off is relatively easy. Any excess glue is removed, three coats of Tung oil are applied to the framework and drawer fronts, sanded and de-nibbed between coats. The sycamore is given two coats of sanding sealer and waxed. The drawer bottoms are left untouched.

Assembly

The two veneered plywood compartment bases can now be glued in, the two secret drawers placed in position, and the top surround glued and screwed in place from underneath.

The hinged lid is then fitted with a flush ring chest fitting and the mirror glued in place with silicon seal to give a slight cushioned effect. With the lid's surround already in place, positioning the hinges is easy – once in place the two stays can be fitted to complete the chest.

Conclusion

On completion I was pleased with the result. Friends remarked on its oriental look – although this was unintentional. It was my first design-and-make project and on reflection I would now do some things differently.

The oak and sycamore have now mellowed harmoniously and regular waxing has improved its overall look. ■

Mackintosh magic

Like many designers at the turn of the 20th century, Charles Rennie Mackintosh was as much an architect as a furniture designer. He planned the exterior of a house to complement the internal furniture and fittings. Mackintosh rarely used surface design on his pieces, preferring to let the shape speak for itself. The library he designed for Glasgow School of Art typifies this. Every element sits together to form a coherent whole – the lights and glazed cupboard panels complement each other, as do the seat backs and table ends. Few rooms look as well 'designed', yet it is as functional as it is pleasing to the eye.

Where decoration was appropriate it was most successfully employed in the form of piercing. Frequently repeated geometric shapes are used to break up door panels, and are echoed in table and chair construction, where jointed strips of wood form patterned ladders. The Willow Tea Room in Glasgow's Sauciehall Street exemplify this sort of decoration.

The dresser was just part of the kitchen refit

The Mackintosh recipe: Part 1

When **Neil McAllister** decided to do up the kitchen of his Edwardian house, he aimed to recapture its original style, while allowing for the needs of modern living

L ike many a grand scheme, doing up the kitchen of our new house had seemed a good idea at first. Much of the rest of the building had escaped the ravages of DIY and retained some wonderful period features.

However, the kitchen had suffered many indignities over 90 years or more. Small and poky and furnished with poor quality 1970s pine units, it would prove an intriguing cabinetmaking and design project. We decided to create a room that embodied the values and characteristics of good Edwardian design, but had the convenience and comfort of a modern kitchen.

From book to reality

Our aim in designing furniture for the kitchen was to blend the best design ideas, that would have been prevalent at the time the house was built, with modern materials and methods. I carried out much research in the library before coming up with a suitable solution. All that remained was for me and my father to put our ideas into practice.

Thinking back to my grandmother's

The kitchen before we started

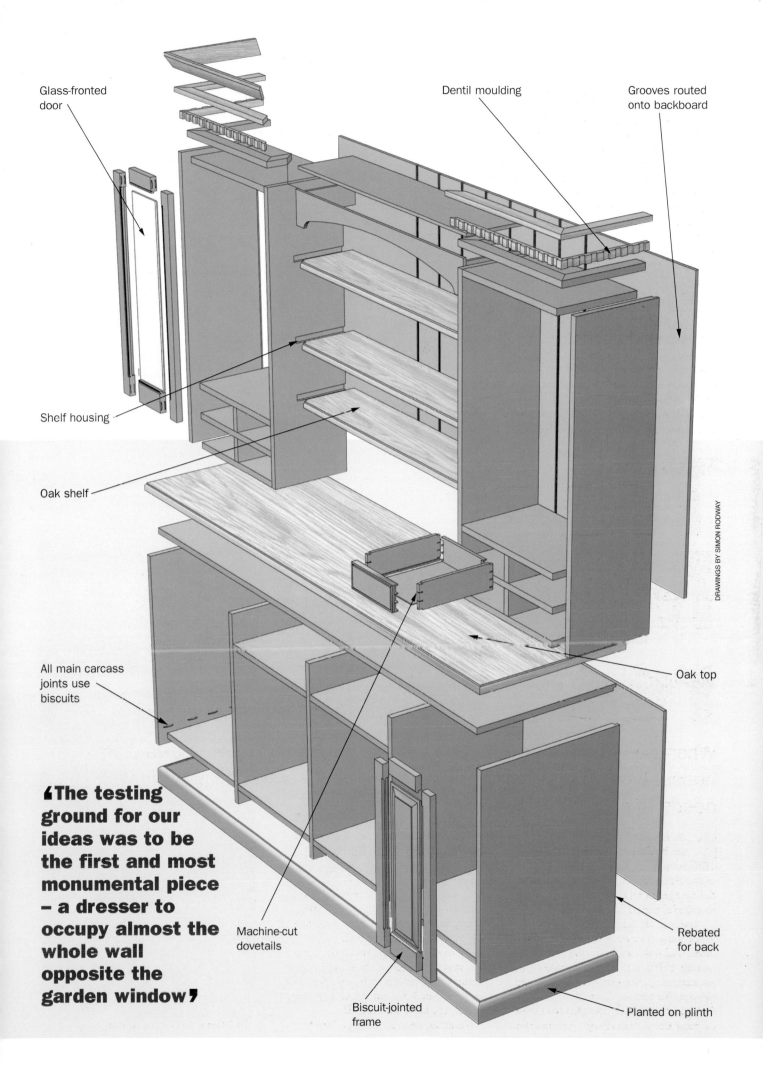

Glass-fronted door

Dentil moulding

Grooves routed onto backboard

Shelf housing

Oak shelf

All main carcass joints use biscuits

Oak top

Machine-cut dovetails

Rebated for back

'The testing ground for our ideas was to be the first and most monumental piece – a dresser to occupy almost the whole wall opposite the garden window'

Biscuit-jointed frame

Planted on plinth

DRAWINGS BY SIMON RODWAY

Assembly is always tricky with such a large object

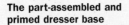

**The part-assembled and
primed dresser base**

Design

Even though I was originally trained in traditional drawing skills, I found the computer my greatest ally in the design stages of the dresser. As the owner of an Apple Mac computer, I used Macromedia Freehand, which, although primarily an illustration package, proved easy to use and flexible enough to produce working drawings for furniture designs.

The computer's ability to 'save as' meant that draft designs could be saved and amended until the right result was reached. I could then print out plans, scaled appropriately for my cabinetmaker (my father) to interpret and turn into three dimensions. I also used the computer to produce same-sized drawings, which we used as templates for some curved components.

For inspiration I looked back at photographs of some splendid dressers by David Lisle, a modern cabinetmaker from Macclesfield. I got more ideas by looking at an assortment of brochures.

Hand-cutting corners of the routed bead of the MDF dresser drawer

Cutting the biscuit joints

and even great-grandmother's kitchen, I remember that the only 'fitted' item was the sink. The rest of it was a jumble of dressers and cupboards, with a kitchen table providing the main 'worktop'. This haphazard style still survives in its original state in a few country houses, and some modern kitchens feature a contemporary interpretation of it.

Castle Drogo, a National Trust property on the fringes of Dartmoor, provided me with inspiration. Designed by Sir Edwin Lutyens, the oak kitchen is simple, yet effective, with plenty of cupboards and worktop space, built round the edges of the room.

Several design sourcebooks provided an idea of the direction in which we should be travelling, and trips to Glasgow and Helensburgh to view

Mackintosh's design ideas also gave us confidence in our task. It seemed that a melding of good design – allied to the Arts and Crafts concept of truth to materials, be they modern or traditional – could be used to create a successful, modern, working kitchen.

Extending the options

When originally built, the space had been two rooms – a kitchen to the side of the house, with a breakfast room to the rear. During the 1960s these rooms had been knocked together, then re-divided to create a side porch, toilet and cloakroom. We built a simple, small single-storey extension beyond the kitchen window, which had a twofold effect – opening up space within the kitchen, and giving the rear elevation of the house a more

Dovetail disasters

We made the two tall cupboards for either side in the same simple way as the base, the only complexity being the addition of four small drawers each to 'close off' the base of each side.

We made drawers from 12mm MDF, with a 25mm face, and machine-cut dovetails. These provided another example of our inexperience with the material. The dovetails had a tendency to flake away – although where they did hold together, as on the fronts, the results were very neat. We disguised any small inaccuracies in construction with fine surface filler.

With such simple construction, some design features were incorporated to break up flat areas. We grooved the drawer front edges to give the appearance of a cot bead. This was achieved simply on the router table, but rather than continue each cut through the edge of the bead and fill the overcut, we decided to stop each cut short and hand-trim the remaining bead. This proved time-consuming, as well as leaving the edges of the drawer open to mechanical damage.

These drawers run on rather unconven-tional plastic runners, glued to the base and sides of the drawer cavity. This has the effect of maintaining the correct space around the drawer front, while protecting the dresser and drawer from wear.

The upper cupboards and shelves sit on an oak worktop, made from four lengths of timber machined to almost 25mm (1in) deep. It is possible to buy ready-made hardwood worktops, but we chose the homemade method. This was a relatively simple job of machining, and biscuit-jointing, although at 2135mm (7ft) long, by 610mm (2ft), it was heavy to handle.

After sanding to remove any surface imperfections, we routed the edge to soften the line and remove the sharp edge. We chose a simple ogee router bit with a very fine cut to avoid an over-ornate edge, which wouldn't have been appropriate for the design.

Flaking dovetails meant that we had to do a bit of filling

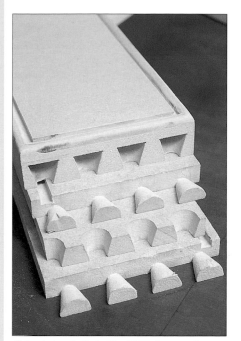

Jig-cut dovetails in the MDF dresser drawer

cohesive and original appearance.

Our first step was to remove the central glazed cupboard, raised on pillars. We then walled the old back passage to create a boiler room, freeing up the space occupied by the former boiler cupboard. What was once a chimney breast was now exposed, creating a recess for a cooker. New girders above the old window allowed the old lower wall to be removed, opening the kitchen into the new bay, with the visual effect of bringing the kitchen into the garden, and extending the room to 7.2m (24ft) long.

Material differences

Now our work could begin. Our original intention had been to build everything using traditional methods, but the scale of the project forced us to compromise on financial grounds. We decided to use traditional materials where possible, but to line cabinet carcasses with wipe-clean melamine-faced board and, where cabinets were to be painted, MDF (medium-density fibreboard).

The testing ground for our ideas was to be the first and most monumental piece – a dresser to occupy almost the whole wall opposite the garden window. The large area to be filled required a design which balanced height and width, without looking inelegant.

Questions of scale

I decided that a painted dresser would look best, so my father and I chose 25mm MDF for the bulk of its

The large area to be filled required a design which balanced height and width, without looking inelegant

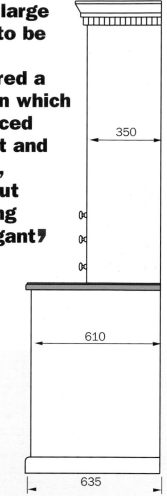

350

610

635

construction. My father is a retired dyer and lifelong amateur cabinetmaker.

Although we have a well-equipped workshop, we found it best to have the sheet material pre-cut accurately, so it required the minimum amount of machining (and dust) in our smallish workshop. However, our decision to biscuit-joint the base showed our inexperience with working with MDF. At over 2.133m (7ft) wide and almost 9.15m (3ft) high, the base was quite a handful to glue and clamp in one go. We had no alternative however, as its closed construction made stage-by-stage gluing-up impossible.

Gluing the biscuit-jointed oak worktop

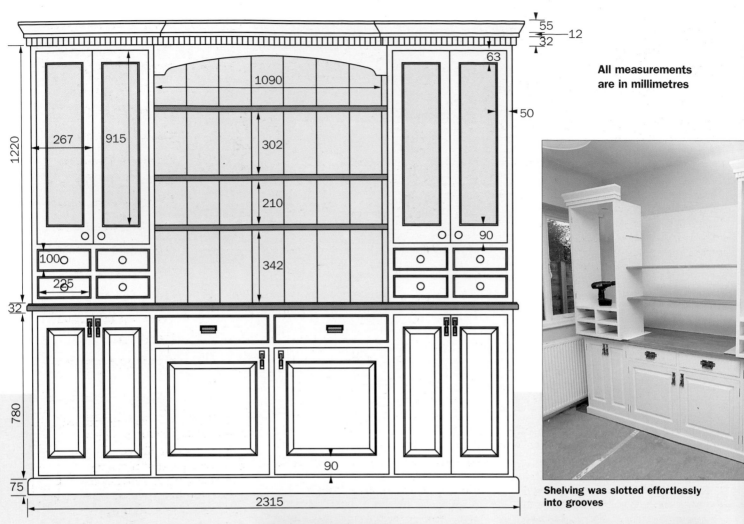

All measurements
are in millimetres

**Shelving was slotted effortlessly
into grooves**

A dry run was essential, so we assembled the carcass as far as possible, and knocked it together to test the accuracy of the cutting and biscuit joints. MDF is not the hardest of materials, which is wonderful when you are working it. However, it requires firm but careful handling to avoid splitting or burring.

Long sash cramps were very useful as we started the assembly, but when we reached the full width, homemade extra-long cramps using Record head and tail stocks had to be employed. The whole assembly was locked into place by a single piece running the length of the top. The base sits directly onto the floor, but the edge is finished with a decorative

The dentil moulding construction

Grooving the back of the dresser with the router

skirting, which gives a satisfyingly solid foot, upon which the dresser stands.

On the shelves

The shelves, simply made from oak, were edged with the same bit, and slotted into grooves recessed in the tall cupboard sides for invisible support. Screws from inside the cupboard hold the shelves firmly, as do fixings through the 9mm (⅜in) MDF backboard.

We had considered making this backboard in the traditional way, using tongue-and-groove pine, but we grooved a single sheet of board with twin parallel routed lines to give us the traditional

A few hinge adjustments were needed when we hung the doors

appearance, along with dimensional stability.

The dresser was topped with a dentil-moulded cornice, which looks stunning. Although this form of moulding is much earlier than the period, this solution proved the strongest.

The moulding is made from five pieces – an MDF base, capped with a plain pine face and angled cornice, which is supported at regular intervals by blocks. The dentil face, which drops a little below the MDF, was created using a homemade router jig, which allowed the work to move through horizontally, while the router passed through on the

A kitchen in which to enjoy good food

'. . . a stroke of luck in our search for appropriate handles for the lower drawers and cupboards as Martin & Co was about to launch a range of handles inspired by the Arts and Crafts movement'

Further reading

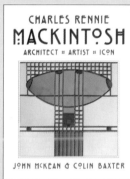

CHARLES RENNIE **MACKINTOSH**
ARCHITECT ☐ ARTIST ☐ ICON

JOHN McKEAN & COLIN BAXTER

Charles Rennie Mackintosh: Architect, Artist, Icon, John McKean & Colin Baxter, £25, Lomond Books 2000, ISBN 0 947 782 08 7. Tel: 0131 551 2261.
Building Traditional Kitchen Cabinets, Jim Tolpin, £14.95, Taunton Press (USA) 1994, ISBN 1 56158 058 9*
Classic Kitchen Projects, Niall Barrett, £17.95, Taunton Press, ISBN 1 56158 386 3*
The Arts & Crafts Movement, Steven Adams, Grange Books 1987
Victorian & Edwardian Furniture, Jeremy Cooper, Thames & Hudson 1987
Liberty Style, Victor Arwas, Rizzoli 1979
The World of Edwardiana, Philippe Gardner, Hamlyn 1974
Edwardian House Style, Hilary Hockman,

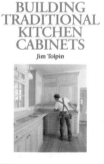

BUILDING TRADITIONAL KITCHEN CABINETS
Jim Tolpin

David & Charles 1994
Gordon Russell, Jeremy Myerson, Design Council 1992
Period Decorating, Mary Gilliatt, Conran Octopus 1990
Period Details, Judith and Martin Miller, Mitchell Beazley 1987
Period Style, Judith and Martin Miller, Mitchell Beazley 1989

* Taunton books are available by mail order from GMC. Tel: 01273 488005

Useful contacts

Arts and Crafts Furniture Company, 49 Sheen Lane, East Sheen, London SW14 8AB. Tel: 020 8876 6544
Bordercraft, Old Forge, Peterchurch, Herefordshire HR2 0SD. Tel: 01981 550251
Fiddes & Son, Florence Works, Brindley Road, Cardiff CF11 8TX. Tel: 029 2034 3235
Hymoor Timber Ltd, Canalside Depot, Newport Lane, Burslem, SOT Tel: 01782 836 636
Martin & Co, 119 Camden Street, Birmingham B1 3DJ. Tel: 0121 233 2111
North Rode Timber, Bark Street, Congleton, Cheshire Tel: 01260 272526
Woodfit, Kem Mill, Whittle-le-Woods, Chorley. Lancs PR6 7EA. Tel: 01257 266421

vertical axis. The slots are achieved by a hinged spacer, which drops into previous cuts, holding the work in place while ensuring regular spacing.

For the lower cupboard doors we used 25mm (1in) MDF frames, surrounding a fielded panel. We glazed the upper cupboard doors with 2mm glass, framing the sight edges with the same routed bead that edges the drawer fronts.

Finishing touches

A degree of pre-painting finishing was needed to ensure a high standard of finish. Sanding sealer, diluted with cellulose thinners, bound the exposed cut edges, and any imperfections were filled with fine surface filler before sanding. We primed the surface, using MDF primer, and used a satin finish paint for kitchens for the finishing coats.

We sourced the wooden knobs for the upper drawers from Woodfit in Chorley, Lancashire, but had a stroke of luck in our search for appropriate handles for the lower drawers and cupboards as Martin & Co was about to launch a range of handles inspired by the Arts and Crafts movement. We selected Mackintosh-inspired drawer pulls and cupboard handles in antiqued brass, which are set off beautifully against the painted finish. These, along with the glass shelves and low-voltage halogen lighting, bring us to the end of Part 1 of our kitchen project. ■

The Mackintosh recipe: Part 2

Having completed the Mackintosh-style dresser,
Neil McAllister and his father now tackle the kitchen cupboards

Our aim in designing new furniture for what was a large, modern kitchen, was not to create a pastiche of Arts and Crafts styles, but to take the best design ideas that would have been prevalent at the time the house was built, and blend them with modern materials and methods.

With our canvas stretched and primed, the proper work could begin. Our original intention was to build everything using traditional cabinetmaking methods, but the scale of the project meant that in the absence of a bottomless wallet, a compromise was

in order. We decided to use traditional materials wherever possible, but for the sake of hygiene, the cabinet carcasses would be lined with melamine-faced board, and when cabinets were to be painted, MDF would be used. This decision was eased during a visit to the Gordon Russell factory in Broadway, where I had learned how creatively MDF can be employed to make quality furniture without an 'MFI look'.

Developing the concept

It soon became evident that our original concept of a kitchen made entirely from

oak, and only employing traditional cabinetmaking techniques, was impractical. Cost was an obvious consideration, because who in their right mind would construct parts never to be seen by human eye from hardwood?

A hundred-year-old kitchen presents other practical problems. Walls that wander in every dimension, floors on three different levels, and some interesting angles – all of which required a pragmatic and practical approach to problem-solving.

Our solution was simple and straightforward. We ordered a lorry-load

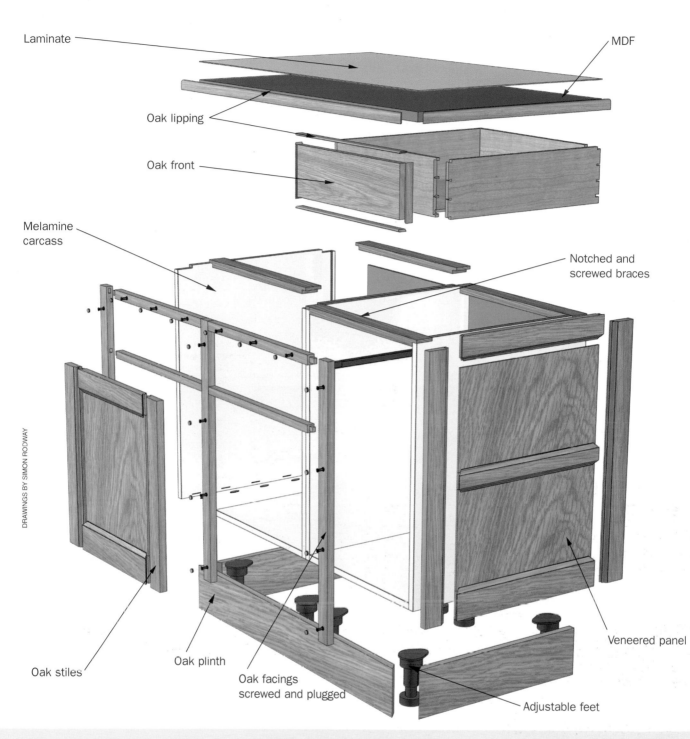

Laminate

MDF

Oak lipping

Oak front

Melamine
carcass

Notched and
screwed braces

DRAWINGS BY SIMON RODWAY

Veneered panel

Oak stiles

Oak plinth

Oak facings
screwed and plugged

Adjustable feet

of magnolia melamine-faced board, from which a series of interlinked carcasses would form the interior of every cupboard. We could have bought flat-pack carcasses, but the size of the kitchen required worktops deeper than standard, and it seemed silly to lose the freedom and flexibility that self-build offered.

Construction
Making the carcasses

Three accurately and cleanly cut pieces, were biscuit-jointed into a 'U' shape. Our own saw copes well when cutting up to 600mm (24in) from panels, so we ordered sheets that were pre-cut to our

specification from a local timber merchant. The back edge of each was grooved on the table saw to allow a cream-faced hardboard panel to slip in and form each cupboard back. As each carcass was cramped, notched spacers ensured that the cabinet stayed square, and diagonal measurements with a pointed stick assisted in this task. Despite our accurate cutting and clamping, a few were initially out of square, but a few choice words, repositioned clamps and some gentle pressure pulled them back into shape.

Cutting the biscuit joints is a simple enough single-handed job with the right tools. While one of us cut, the other

ensured good positioning, using the try square to achieve a square cut. It is possible to do this single-handed, but we found that two people were able to complete the task in a quarter of the time.

Fluctuating floor levels made adjustable feet a must. The fine-tuning of the cabinet's height also allowed us to make a clip-fit kickboard. The individual units were then fitted together, and secured to the wall to form a very solid structure.

Visitors during the earliest stages, who knew of the project's aim, were a little put off by the underlying construction, but our aim was to provide a strong, hygienic structure capable of

Testing the cabinet for square

Using a try-square to ensure accurate biscuit jointing

Assembling the melamine carcasses

Creating a paper template to cut the worktop laminate accurately

accommodating built-in appliances, and yet invisibly carrying services such as power, water and drainage. We wanted something modern and practical, yet still capable of being transformed into a traditional cabinet-made kitchen.

Worktops

The carcasses were topped with shaped 25mm (1in) MDF worktops, which were very carefully sealed to prevent water ingress. These were then made practical with a Formica surface. These days, a wide variety of work surfaces are available, ranging from the 'bog-standard' post-formed items on sale at your local DIY warehouse, to composite

or stone marvels, which cost as much as an Aston Martin. We chose Formica for all the reasons that it has become such an established favourite over the years. It is hard-wearing, flexible, reasonably easy to work with, and is available in a staggering variety of finishes. If we had remained true to our original design ideal, we would have either used unfinished oak or painted wood – but just how authentic do you have to be? At that level, we might as well bring back rickets, child labour and gas lighting! After all, some progress has been good – so Formica it was!

Some very complex shapes that entailed tricky cutting were required, and

so pieces that butted up against walls or window frames were cut precisely to shape, using paper templates. Sheets of heavy paper were cut slightly small, then held flat to the MDF top. Smaller strips were then carefully trimmed and stuck down, butting the adjoining surfaces, to form a very accurate cutting template.

This was then stuck down with clear Sellotape to the Formica, which was first rough-cut with a very fine jigsaw blade (ensuring that the work was supported firmly near the cut edge to avoid splitting). Fine trimming was then done with a Goscut. I doubt if this design wonder from the 1960s is still in manufacture, but it works wonderfully

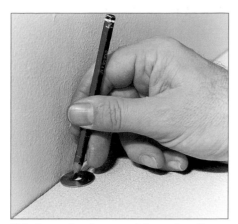

Using a washer to accurately mark wall profile onto laminate

Thin wood spacers support the laminate during positioning

Using a Goscut to cut laminate to shape

❝I employed an unconventional, but very accurate technique for scribing the contours of an uneven wall onto the laminate❞

Spreading contact adhesive

well, like a miniature guillotine, cutting or nibbling away without chipping.

Scribing

I employed an unconventional, but very accurate technique for scribing the contours of an uneven wall onto the laminate. Using a small washer and pencil, I was able to run the pencil along the wall, giving a perfectly accurate line to cut along. This technique was obviously only of use for the rear of long worktops, as the cut is offset by the depth of the washer.

The laminate was fixed traditionally using contact adhesive, with thin strips of wood being essential to hold both surfaces apart and allow controlled fixing in precise position. The edges were well rolled down, and further sealed with coloured laminate filler, to keep out moisture and achieve a seamless finish. The edge trailing over the MDF was then trimmed with a router, and finished with an oak trim.

Oak carcass facing

Each cabinet was then faced with a traditionally made oak skeleton, from which all cupboard doors were to be

hung, and through which the drawers would run on pre-fitted runners. This way of working required accurate measuring, jointing, fixing and hinge rebating, but meant that the finished appearance gave no clue to the underlying framework.

The oak frame is made slightly wider than the carcass it covers, to ensure a tidy appearance. It is fixed using glue and recessed screws, and disguised using plugs cut from the same timber. Both plugs and recessed holes are best cut on a pillar drill, to ensure the plug fits snugly.

The drawers are made from beech as a closed box construction, with hand-cut dovetails, and a routed outer edge for a softer appearance. My father preferred this method of dovetail cutting to machining, as he used a quirky, yet quick and accurate method of setting up the cuts.

Drawers

The drawer fascia were made from a single piece of planed oak, trimmed with an oak beading slightly deeper at the front and rear, which gave a hard-wearing and attractive finished edge. The beading was simply made in lengths on

the router and saw tables, then cut to size on a mitre guillotine. A power saw or a hand mitre saw would be just as effective. The 'frame' of beading was then glued to the drawer front, using a piece of thick card to maintain the degree of offset, and a string clamp to hold everything tight during gluing.

By constructing and fitting the beech drawer first, the oak fascia could then be retro-fitted to ensure its perfect position within the frame. This speeded up the usually time-consuming drawer fitting process.

Cupboard doors continued the theme of simplicity, with an oak frame construction containing a plain panel of oak-faced MDF. We used a two-part rail and stile cutter on the router table to construct the doors. For those readers who haven't used this kind of cutter, it speeds up door making and, accurately set up, yields very clean results. The first cut is made using one cutter, and then the second cutter is set up using scraps of waste timber and adjusted to give an accurate cut, which fits perfectly into the first joint. The male and female cuts are then glued together with the centre panel slotted in.

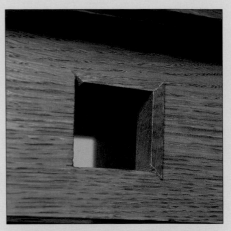

Fitting external oak face to carcasses

Fitting 25mm MDF worktop into window bay

Trimming excess laminate with router

Applying moulding to square decorative hole

Square decorative hole on the door panels

Panels

Traditionally the panel is left unglued, free to expand or contract. To prevent the panel rattling, we used rubber Palalign strips, from the Woodcut Trading Company. These sit into the rebate, compress when the frame is glued together and provide firm, flexible hold for the panel insert.

Allowance has to be made for these inserts when cutting the panel. Make the 5mm (¼in) strip compress to 2.5mm (⅛in), by deducting 5mm (¼in) off each dimension of the panel. The same technique is used to make glazed panels, with the rear part of the rebate cut away before assembly, to allow the glass to be fitted, after which it is secured with a small oak bead.

The two exposed end panels were closed off in oak with two-part panels, made in similar manner to the cupboard doors, and fixed with countersunk screws from inside the cupboard.

In making the panels and cupboard doors, we followed the design principle that the bottom rail is wider than the top rail and stiles. This convention is also widely used in art, when mounting pictures. Having a deeper base, gives the

door a settled, balanced appearance, as if the rest of the door has something to sit on, which sounds bizarre but really works.

Door hanging

As readers will realise, hanging one door is a time-consuming task, hanging a kitchen-full would take forever. Almost all modern fitted kitchens use sprung cabinet hinges, which sit into a 35mm (1⅜in) hole in the carcass, and then connect onto plates attached to the door. These have the advantage of being self-closing, and are very adjustable. Despite this we finally decided to use polished brass butt hinges to achieve a more traditional appearance.

The rebates were pre-routed into the rails before they were assembled, and it is a relatively simple job to mark and rebate the door edge, either using a commercially available router guide, or, like us, a homemade device. This simple creation is basically an oversized rectangular hole, which clamps to the work. A router, set to the right depth of cut, is simply run inside the hole, which is dimensioned to take account of the bit's collar. A few quick chisel cuts clean

off the rounded corners, and *voilà* – a prefect hinge rebate. The template has to be set correctly, as does the router depth, but properly set up, the job takes a minute or so per rebate and produces a very clean resulting cut.

Furniture and fixings

The simple pulls for the drawer fronts were from Martin & Co. These are available in an antique finish, but I was a little shocked on opening the packet, as the handles looked like finds from an archaeological dig! However, a controlled buff with Autosol metal polish created just the right amount of shine, while still leaving enough patina for an authentic appearance. Two coats of lacquer protected my handiwork, and the pulls were fixed using similarly antiqued dome-headed screws, remembering to keep all the screw slots horizontal for a uniform, finished appearance.

Oak is a beautiful wood, but it needs brass screws as its tannic acid quickly rusts steel and will stain the wood black. A simple mistake made by beginners is to pre-drill then fix directly with a brass screw. In the best case, the screw head

Homemade jig for routing hinge rebates

The drawer fascia and the beading were made from solid oak

Further reading

Charles Rennie Mackintosh: Architect, Artist, Icon, John McKean & Colin Baxter, £25, Lomond Books 2000, ISBN 0 947 782 08 7. Tel: 0131 551 2261.

Building Traditional Kitchen Cabinets, Jim Tolpin, £14.95,Taunton Press (USA) 1994, ISBN 1 56158 058 9 gmc✓

Classic Kitchen Projects, Niall Barrett, £17.95, Taunton Press, ISBN 1 56158 386 3 gmc✓

The Arts & Crafts Movement, Steven Adams, Grange Books 1987

Victorian & Edwardian Furniture, Jeremy Cooper, Thames & Hudson 1987

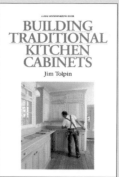

Liberty Style, Victor Arwas, Rizzoli 1979
The World of Edwardiana, Philippe Gardner, Hamlyn 1974
Edwardian House Style, Hilary Hockman, David & Charles 1994
Gordon Russell, Jeremy Myerson, Design Council 1992
Period Decorating, Mary Gilliatt, Conran Octopus 1990
Period Details, Judith and Martin Miller, Mitchell Beazley 1987
Period Style, Judith and Martin Miller, Mitchell Beazley 1989

gmc✓ Taunton books are available by mail order from GMC. Tel: 01273 488005

Useful contacts

Arts and Crafts Furniture Company, 49 Sheen Lane, East Sheen, London SW14 8AB. Tel: 020 8876 6544
Bordercraft, Old Forge, Peterchurch, Herefordshire HR2 0SD. Tel: 01981 550251
Fiddes & Son, Florence Works, Brindley Road, Cardiff CF11 8TX. Tel: 029 2034 3235
Hymoor Timber Ltd, Canalside Depot, Newport Lane, Burslem, SOT. Tel: 01782 836 636
Martin & Co, 119 Camden Street, Birmingham B1 3DJ. Tel: 0121 233 2111
North Rode Timber, Bark Street, Congleton, Cheshire Tel: 01260 272526
Woodfit, Kem Mill, Whittle-le-Woods, Chorley, Lancs PR6 7EA. Tel: 01257 266421
The Woodcut Trading Co., 80 Ninfield Rd, Sidley, Bexhill-on-Sea, E. Sussex TN39 5BB. Tel: 01424 819909

Antiqued brass pulls before and after buffing

burrs, in the worst it snaps. Piloting with a steel screw of the same size will allow the brass screw to seat cleanly and without damage.

Appliances

The fitted dishwasher and fridge are disguised by panels that match their neighbours. The dishwasher has the appearance of a drawer with a cupboard below, but is attached to the appliance to open from the top. This was slightly problematic to make, as, even though the cabinet is deeper than normal, a thinner door had to be made so it would lay flush with the rest of the doors.

Finishing

We needed a durable, yet attractive finish for all the exposed oak, preferring a soft mellow appearance. Fiddes' finishes proved to be just the job, with a complete range for the cabinetmaker.

After a very light stain, which added a little warmth to the bare oak, three coats of satin clear glaze were applied, with each being lightly rubbed down with 0000 wire wool, to knock off any 'nibs', and then dusted, vacuumed and wiped with a rag before the next was applied. The manufacturer recommends 4–6 hours between coats.

The finished wood was left with a rather unnatural, but very durable, finish, which we then rubbed down with Vita Shine, applied with a cloth. This is a kind of waxy cutting paste which, as well as burnishing the varnish or lacquer to a silky sheen, cleans the wood. Any excess is immediately wiped off in the direction of the grain with a clean, absorbent cloth. After 15 minutes it is dry enough to buff. A second application is rarely required on new wood. Two coatings of wax gave the wood a really appealing furniture-quality finish, which was warm and waxy to the touch.

The cupboard doors all use sanded oak knobs, with magnetic catches – a practical solution with the right visual appearance, but it was fortunate that I bought a few more than I needed. The knobs in the first batch were stained and given two coats of varnish before fitting. A third coat of varnish would be applied to the whole door. The lighting of the room is sufficiently varied, however, so that some knobs appeared exactly the right shade and some were too dark. Varnishing some plain, unstained knobs gave me a number of lighter alternatives, which could be swapped with the darker versions to achieve a tonal match. ■

The Mackintosh recipe: Part 3

In the previous part, **Neil McAllister's** Arts and Crafts kitchen was taking shape, and in this final article Neil and his father create cabinets with character to finish the job

A long expanse of worktop along the kitchen's left wall required a variety of units providing drawer and cupboard space, but with sufficient diversity to look interesting. The wine rack, with capacity for 20 bottles, takes the place of a conventional cupboard and is simply constructed.

The neck supports are made from 25 x 90mm (1 x 3½in) oak, in which five 45mm (1¾in) holes are cleanly bored. When sawn in half along its length, this yields two lengths of neck supports.

The back of the bottle could have been supported by a similar arrangement with larger holes, but it was easier to rest the back of the bottle on a strip of 25mm (1in) wood, and employ simple triangles to prevent the bottle from moving.

These strips are fixed with countersunk screws from the adjacent cupboards. As they are set back into the carcass, the exposed melamine surface is disguised with a thin sheet of oak.

I was keen to ensure that the kitchen had a cohesive appearance, without every unit being identical. We achieved this by changing certain design elements, while keeping others common. This side of the kitchen features two of the most successful parts, the bookcase/dresser and plate rack. As the kitchen has a separate, yet linked, eating area, the first cabinet is built continuously into the run of units, but looks like a tall bookcase, with cupboards below. To achieve this appearance, the line of drawers stops at two full-height cupboard doors. Rising

All the trimmings

Mackintosh used pierced geometric shapes in his designs, and these have been reinterpreted by a number of modern makers. I used four squares, cut in a square pattern to draw the eye towards the handles and break up what could otherwise have been a monotonously plain panel. In our early experiments we simply used square cuts, but these appeared raw. My father used some nimble table-saw technique to make a length of tiny L-shaped moulding, which, once cut on the mitre guillotine, sat in the hole, and overlapped the edge of the panel. Such a fiddly job may seem unnecessary, but small features such as this transform the ordinary into the extraordinary – as well as assisting in my scheme to keep my father from idleness!

Martin & Co. came up trumps again with handles from its 'Mission' Arts and Crafts range. These have the rustic appearance of beaten, antiqued brass, which suited the style of this cabinet and continued the theme of the whole kitchen.

Applying moulding to the decorative square hole on the top face rail of the plate rack

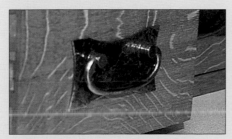
This Arts and Crafts-style handle from Martin & Co. suited the theme admirably

The completed moulding on the decorative square

The separate bookcase

Cornice detail on the bookcase

from the worktop, four small drawers sit below a tall bookcase.

Simple lines

The bookcase is simple in its lines and, unlike the previously described cabinets, is made using more traditional methods with panelled sides, hand-dovetailed oak drawers and oak shelves. The main design feature of the upper cabinet is the particularly wide, flat cornice, fielded with a raised panel cutter, and applied as a decorative rather than a structural element. This sort of feature regularly appears in Arts and Crafts work, as an elegant antidote to the twiddly, ornate Gothic style of mid-Victorian furniture. We spotted a very pleasant example in an antique shop, which guided our own approach.

Inspired by Castle Drogo

The final cabinet on this side of the kitchen is also the most unusual in design and proved to be the hardest to construct. This was originally to be a simple wall cabinet – but, inspired by Castle Drogo's immense plate rack, we created a bold design with a raised, pierced central panel.

The central section is conventionally constructed using biscuit joints, but unlike the bookcase, the cornice is integral rather than an attached decoration. It also has an extended bottom panel, which forms the base of the side cupboards. The central divider for the plate rods is also fixed with biscuits, and has holes pre-bored to accommodate the rods. With both upper and lower sections the upper bars are bored right through and the

lower ones halfway. This allows the rods to be inserted and withdrawn at will in case of breakage, or for cleaning.

Side cupboards

The side cupboards are less conventional – each top and side are pre-joined in an L-shape, taking care to keep the join at 90°. In a tricky manoeuvre, they are attached to the central section, and clamped top and bottom using long sash cramps at the same time that the bottom cornice is attached. It doesn't take a genius to realise that making it this way requires some very strange clamping, but fortunately we were able to get the whole thing glued, solid and square.

Fixing by just using cabinet hangers at the top of the central unit would have placed an unnecessary strain on the side

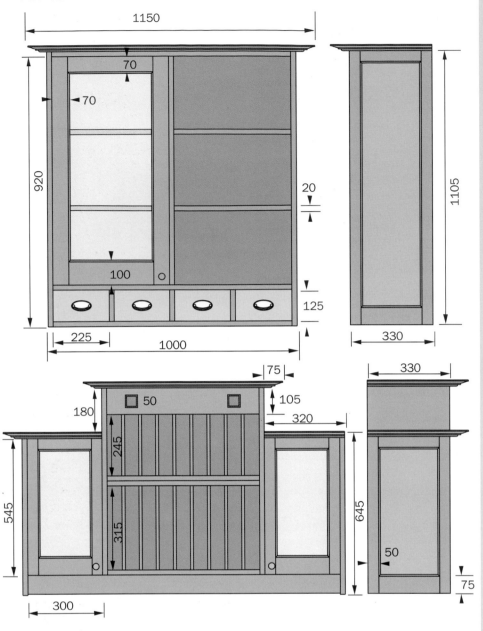

All measurements are in millimetres

Shades of oak

It is advisable before staining oak, to damp the surface in order to raise the grain, then sand it again before applying the stain. This may be largely unnecessary when using Naptha stains, as they don't seem to raise the grain.

Rather than buy small tins of stain, some suppliers sell quality stains in trade quantities, at only a little more cost than small DIY tins. Before we pressed him into servitude as our personal cabinetmaker, my father was a professional colourist in the textile industry. A working lifetime's knowledge of colour-mixing theory and practice proved very useful in this project.

In the end, we mixed equal parts of Light Oak and Golden Oak, diluted with thinners to achieve the pale shade we required. We tested various mixtures in small quantities on a small piece of scrap timber, labelling it with the recipe. A good general rule is to mix sufficient stain to complete the job. But providing you have worked with reasonable accuracy, you can always mix to the same recipe.

❝ The bookcase is simple in its lines and, unlike the previously described cabinets, is made using more traditional methods . . .❞

cupboards. We used four additional fixings along the back bar, to spread the load across the whole cabinet and help prevent the biscuit joints at the top of each side bearing too much stress.

A design feature popular among some handmade kitchens, is the fireplace-style cooker surround. We had a real fireplace in which we could place our range. We are not quite posh – or rich – enough for an Aga, but we found a superb cooker, intended for professional kitchens, just the right size and appearance for our aperture – it also bakes great oven chips!

Refined design

The cooker protrudes a few inches from the wall, so the line of painted MDF cabinets takes its line from the cooker handles, which means that the flanking

drawers and cupboards are only a few inches deep! We could have used false drawers, but just for fun made conventional, but very shallow, beech drawers. These are just big enough to hold a pair of oven gloves, but have an irritating way of falling out every time we forget they are only four inches deep! The two cupboards to the right occupy the entire depth of the chimney-breast. The whole assembly is made in pre-cut 25mm (1in) MDF, biscuit-jointed on-site, and simply finished with plain cupboard doors.

We made a distinct design improvement by framing the drawer fronts with pine beading, in a similar style to the oak drawers, rather than routing a mock bead, as on the dresser. This is far easier to make and much more hard-wearing. It

is not integral to the actual beech drawer, but is fixed as a decorative front.

Focal point

This part of the kitchen is crowned by the painted mantel, which was simplicity itself to make, but is a very effective and highly visible focal point. The frame is made with plain MDF panels using the two-part rail and stile cutter. The outer edges are left plain, and the whole assembly sits comfortably on the flanking cabinets.

The mantelshelf is made in two parts from 25mm (1in) MDF, the first, a conventional shelf, sitting on three shaped brackets. These were first cut to shape on a scrollsaw, then the edges were rounded on the router table. The mantel is capped with a similar fielded cornice to the

Dovetailed drawers are on runners

The rest of the kitchen, with mantel surround and more painted MDF units, including a separate island unit

Biscuit-jointed mitre

Solid top

Glass

Veneered panel

Solid shelves

Solid base

Dovetailed drawer construction

Routed groove for runners

Solid division

Rebated for base

Drawer runners screwed back and front

bookcase and plate rack, but with a shallower cut from the raised panel cutter. This cornice prevents plates from slipping, and elegantly caps the 'fireplace'.

This, like the dresser, is finished in Dulux Satinwood, and even in heavy wear areas near the cooker, is not yet showing any markings or discolouration.

Some manufacturers artificially age painted pieces like this, using scumble or varnish, which in the right kitchen can be very effective, especially when new furniture needs to sit alongside older cabinets. This sort of distressing can result in a stained, grubby appearance, so we chose to keep it looking clean.

Oak worktop

A similar oak worktop to the large dresser, made of four planks biscuit-jointed together, completes this unit, but

the wall's similarity to a dog's hind leg meant that a perfect fit, butting up to the wall, wasn't possible. We were left with a tiny gap to fill along a wavy wall. A simple, flexible oak moulding provided the solution.

A rounded edge was routed onto a 35mm (1⅜in) plank, which was then sawn off at around 6mm (¼in) thick. This was stuck to the wall and worktop using a 'No More Nails' type adhesive, which provided a clean, watertight edge to all the kitchen's work surfaces.

The final cabinet was a compromise between 21st-century practicality and Edwardian authenticity. Being such a large kitchen, with 8ft between the cooker and opposite work surface, this provided a central work area with storage below and power supply for those essential electrical appliances our Edwardian

predecessors couldn't even imagine. The basis of the structure was three interlinked melamine-covered carcasses, which formed one wide cupboard opposite the sink, and another long cupboard accessible both from the cooker and work surface side.

Using the same carcass construction, and 'Woodfit' adjustable legs, these were screwed together via their fixing battens. Melamine-to-melamine surfaces were drilled through and fixed using standard carcass connectors. Then, to ensure total rigidity, battens were screwed on the underside.

Bookcase

The unit features a bookcase at the table end, which is made conventionally from oak (*Quercus* spp). It requires some fine-tolerance cabinetmaking, as it slips

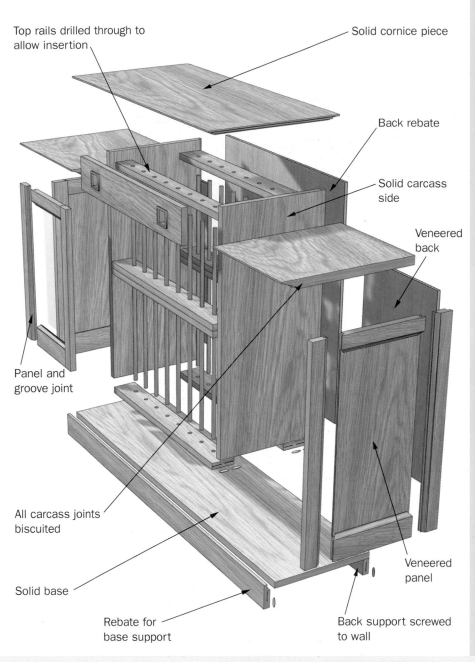

Top rails drilled through to allow insertion

Solid cornice piece

Back rebate

Solid carcass side

Veneered back

Panel and groove joint

All carcass joints biscuited

Solid base

Rebate for base support

Back support screwed to wall

Veneered panel

Sources

Fiddes & Son,
Florence Works, Brindley Road,
Cardiff CF11 8TX. Tel: 029 2034 3235
Hymoor Timber Ltd,
Canalside Depot, Newport Lane, Burslem,
SOT. Tel: 01782 836 636
Martin & Co.,
119 Camden Street, Birmingham B1 3DJ.
Tel: 0121 233 2111
North Rode Timber,
Bark Street, Congleton, Cheshire.
Tel: 01260 272526.
Woodfit,
Kem Mill, Whittle-le-Woods, Chorley, Lancs
PR6 7EA. Tel: 01257 266421

The finished cabinets in situ

precisely onto the carcass, is fixed with screws from the inside, and its weight is supported by two adjustable legs.

It sounds as if this should be a weak attachment, but it is a very solid part of the structure. Before fitting, the rear stiles were rebated to accommodate the door hinge.

The rest of the non-opening parts are clad in two panels with extra-deep top rails, into which electrical sockets are fitted.

Before these were fixed, the outer edge of one stile and the back of the other were rebated for door hinges. Once screwed on from inside, these panels were solid enough to hang the cupboard doors from.

Space to work

We used 25mm (1in) MDF for the

worktop, which was covered with laminate and trimmed in oak, like the rest of the oak units, providing the kitchen with a very useful central surface, extending the famous 'work triangle' of cooker, fridge and sink, into a work square. This proves especially useful when serving and preparing food, as a 90° turn from the cooker reveals over 2sq m of horizontal surface.

Down to earth

Our final trauma came in finding flooring which showed off the kitchen's materials, but was practical and inexpensive. We managed to find something that fulfilled all but the last requirement. Amtico is like upmarket lino, laid in tiles and strips on a plywood base.

The final choice, grey-blue slate streaked with tan, sounds dreadful, but

looks divine, complementing the oak's warm tone and the painted cabinets, while looking natural and organic.

The finished kitchen looks superb. It is practical and homely, as much a living room as a kitchen, and will always be a testament to my father's woodworking skills and patience – for which we will always be grateful.

People have asked if we would undertake such a mammoth task again. It was tremendously hard work, and although the cost wasn't small, there is no way we could have afforded to have something so beautiful made by professionals, nor could we have bought a flat-pack kitchen to fit so perfectly. So, the answer is yes! The project has been a resounding success. We have a real one-off kitchen, worthy of the house, which fulfils our original intention. ∎

Conversion table:
inches to millimetres

inch		mm	inch		mm
1/64	0.0565	0.3969	1/2	0.500	12.700
1/32	0.03125	0.7938	33/64	0.515625	13.0969
3/64	0.046875	1.1906	17/32	0.53125	13.4938
1/16	0.0625	1.5875	35/64	0.546875	13.8906
			9/16	0.5625	14.2875
5/64	0.078125	1.9844			
3/32	0.09375	2.3812	37/64	0.578125	14.6844
7/64	0.109375	2.7781	19/32	0.59375	15.0812
			39/64	0.609375	15.4781
1/8	0.125	3.1750			
9/64	0.140625	3.5719	5/8	0.625	15.8750
5/32	0.15625	3.9688	41/64	0.640625	16.2719
11/64	0.171875	4.3656	21/32	0.65625	16.6688
			43/64	0.671875	17.0656
3/16	0.1875	4.7625	11/16	0.6875	17.4625
13/64	0.203125	5.1594	45/64	0.703125	17.8594
7/32	0.21875	5.5562	23/32	0.71875	18.2562
15/64	0.234375	5.9531			
1/4	0.250	6.3500	47/64	0.734375	18.6531
17/64	0.265625	6.7469	3/4	0.750	19.0500
9/32	0.28125	7.5406			
5/16	0.3125	7.9375	49/64	0.765625	19.4469
			25/32	0.78125	19.8438
21/64	0.1328125	8.3344	51/64	0.796875	20.2406
11/32	0.34375	8.7312	13/16	0.8125	20.6375
23/64	0.359375	9.1281			
			53/64	0.828125	21.0344
3/8	0.375	9.5250	27/32	0.84375	21.0344
25/64	0.390625	9.9219	55/64	0.858375	21.8281
13/32	0.40625	10.3188			
27/64	0.421875	10.7156	7/8	0.875	22.2250
			57/64	0.890625	22.6219
7/16	0.4375	11.1125	29/32	0.90625	23.0188
29/64	0.453125	11.5094	59/64	0.921875	23.4156
15/32	0.46875	11.9062			
31/64	0.484375	12.3031	15/16	0.9375	23.8125
			61/64	0.953125	24.2094
			31/32	0.96875	24.6062
			63/64	0.984375	25.0031
			1	1.00	25.4

Index

a

acrylic varnish	36
adhesives	
application	23, 33, 82–3
slower setting	34
American timber	65
Amtico flooring	118
Applegate, Mark: five-drawer oak and sycamore chest	
	59–64
Arts & Crafts influenced projects	
cabinet	47–52
clothes chest	91–5
Mackintosh-style kitchen	
Part 1	102–7
Part 2	108–13
Part 3	114–18
ash	42
and Danish oil	15

b

baize, attaching to board	34
Barnsley, Edward	91
Bichromium of Potash	63
Bullar, John: Arts & Crafts style cabinet	47–52

c

Cabinetmaking – The Professional Approach (Alan Peters)	
	70
cabinets	
Arts & Crafts style	47–52
breakfront	65–70
corner cabinet in English cherry	2–7
display cabinet in oak and walnut	53–8
hi-fi	77–81
mahogany side cabinet	32–7
oak display cabinet	26–31
TV	
Part 1	82–6
Part 2	87–90
see also Mackintosh-style kitchen	
Cascamite	34
Castle Drogo, Devon	104, 115
CD storage	
CD rack	38–41
hi-fi cabinet	77–81
Charlesworth, David	93
chests of drawers	
clothes chest with Arts & Crafts influence	91–5
English oak and sycamore	96–101
five-drawer oak and sycamore	59–64
limed	13–16
for a master bedroom	42–6
Constanduros, Mark: glazed oak sideboard	8–12
corner cabinet in English cherry	2–7
Cowie, Mike	
kitchen dresser with angled legs and burr	
Part 1	17–21
Part 2	22–5
limed chest of drawers	13–16
TV cabinet	
Part 1	82–6
Part 2	87–90
curves, cutting	80

d

Danish oil	4, 7, 21, 52, 70, 90
and ash	15
Davies, Stanley	94
Devitt-Spooner, Brendan	
breakfront cabinet	65–70
corner cabinet in English cherry	2–7
display cabinet in oak and walnut	53–8
display cabinets	
oak	26–31
oak and walnut	53–8
dovetails	16, 21, 44, 50–1, 63, 83, 105
dressers	
with angled legs and burr	
Part 1	17–21
Part 2	22–5
Mackintosh-style	102–7
traditional	71–6

e

elm	17, 47–50
English walnut	47

f

fabrics, attaching to board	34
Fiddes' finishes	33, 113
finishes	
Bichromium of Potash	63
Danish oil	4, 7, 21, 52, 70, 90
and ash	15
Fiddes' finishes	33, 113
heat resistant	36
Liberon Finishing Oil	81
Naptha stains	116
Nitrostain	12
painted	117
Rustin's acrylic varnish	36
Rustin's Plastic Coating	36
sprays	40
staining oak	116
Vaseline	7, 57
Vita Shine	113
Formica worktops	110–11

g

glass	
cutting	88
handmade look	25
glue	
application	23, 33, 82–3
slower setting	34
Gullam, Phillip: traditional dresser	71–6

h

handles	7
Arts & Crafts style	107, 115, 117
brass	12, 37, 101, 107, 112, 115, 117
wood	31, 95, 113
heat resistant finishes	36
hi-fi cabinet Kortright, David	77–81

Index

i

inlays 6, 40

k

kitchen, Mackintosh-style
    Part 1 102–7
    Part 2 108–13
    Part 3 114–18
kitchen dressers see dressers
Kortright, David: hi-fi cabinet 77–81

l

Lawton, Andrew: clothes chest with Arts & Crafts influence
91–5
Lentge, Roswitha and Jeff Smith: oak display cabinet
26–31
Liberon Finishing Oil 81
limed chest of drawers 13–16
liming techniques 15–16
Lisle, David 104
Lyall, Duncan: English oak and sycamore chest of drawers
96–101

m

Mackintosh, Charles Rennie 102, 107
Mackintosh-style kitchen
    Part 1 102–7
    Part 2 108–13
    Part 3 114–18
Macromedia Freehand 104
McAllister, Neil: Mackintosh-style kitchen
    Part 1 102–7
    Part 2 108–13
    Part 3 114–18

n

Naptha stains 116
Nitrostain 12

o

oak
    liming 15–16
    screws for 112–13
    staining 116
olive ash 42

p

painted finishes 117
Palalign strips 112
pivot pins (hinging method) 52
Plastic Coating 36
pocket doors 84
projects
    cabinets
        Arts & Crafts style 47–52
        breakfront 65–70
        corner cabinet in English cherry 2–7
        display cabinet in oak and walnut 53–8
        hi-fi 77–81

        mahogany side cabinet 32–7
        oak display cabinet 26–31
        TV
            Part 1 82–6
            Part 2 87–90
    CD rack 38–41
    chests of drawers
        clothes chest with Arts & Crafts influence 91–5
        English oak and sycamore 96–101
        five-drawer oak and sycamore 59–64
        limed 13–16
        for a master bedroom 42–6
    dressers
        with angled legs and burr
            Part 1 17–21
            Part 2 22–5
        Mackintosh-style 102–7
        traditional 71–6
    kitchen in Mackintosh-style
        Part 1 102–7
        Part 2 108–13
        Part 3 114–18
    sideboard, glazed oak 8–12
putty 88

r

Ripley, Mark: chest of drawers for a master bedroom
42–6
Rustin's acrylic varnish 36
Rustin's Plastic Coating 36

s

sapwood 65
side cabinet 32–7
sideboard, glazed oak 8–12
Smith, Derek: CD rack 38–41
Smith, Jeff and Roswitha Lentge: oak display cabinet
26–31
stringing 60

t

Technique of Furniture Making (Ernest Joyce) 95
timber 14
    American 65
    waney edged 97
TV cabinet
    Part 1 82–6
    Part 2 87–90

v

varnish, acrylic 36
Vaseline 7, 57
veneering 10, 86
vacuum-bag press 85, 86

w

walnut, English 47
waney edged timber 97
white ash 42
Wilson, Harold: mahogany side cabinet 32–7
worktops 76, 110–11, 118

TITLES AVAILABLE FROM
GMC Publications

BOOKS

WOODCARVING

Beginning Woodcarving	GMC Publications
Carving Architectural Detail in Wood: The Classical Tradition	
Frederick Wilbur	
Carving Birds & Beasts	GMC Publications
Carving the Human Figure: Studies in Wood and Stone	
	Dick Onians
Carving Nature: Wildlife Studies in Wood	Frank Fox–Wilson
Carving on Turning	Chris Pye
Celtic Carved Lovespoons: 30 Patterns	Sharon Littley & Clive Griffin
Decorative Woodcarving (New Edition)	Jeremy Williams
Elements of Woodcarving	Chris Pye
Essential Woodcarving Techniques	Dick Onians
Figure Carving in Wood: Human and Animal Forms	
	Sara Wilkinson
Lettercarving in Wood: A Practical Course	Chris Pye
Relief Carving in Wood: A Practical Introduction	Chris Pye
Woodcarving for Beginners	GMC Publications
Woodcarving Made Easy	Cynthia Rogers
Woodcarving Tools, Materials & Equipment	
(New Edition in 2 vols.)	Chris Pye

WOODTURNING

Bowl Turning Techniques Masterclass	Tony Boase
Chris Child's Projects for Woodturners	Chris Child
Contemporary Turned Wood: New Perspectives in a Rich Tradition	
	Ray Leier, Jan Peters & Kevin Wallace
Decorating Turned Wood: The Maker's Eye	
	Liz & Michael O'Donnell
Green Woodwork	Mike Abbott
Intermediate Woodturning Projects	GMC Publications
Keith Rowley's Woodturning Projects	Keith Rowley
Making Screw Threads in Wood	Fred Holder
Segmented Turning: A Complete Guide	Ron Hampton
Turned Boxes: 50 Designs	Chris Stott
Turning Green Wood	Michael O'Donnell
Turning Pens and Pencils	Kip Christensen & Rex Burningham
Woodturning: Forms and Materials	John Hunnex
Woodturning: A Foundation Course (New Edition)	Keith Rowley
Woodturning: A Fresh Approach	Robert Chapman
Woodturning: An Individual Approach	Dave Regester
Woodturning: A Source Book of Shapes	John Hunnex
Woodturning Masterclass	Tony Boase
Woodturning Techniques	GMC Publications

WOODWORKING

Beginning Picture Marquetry	Lawrence Threadgold
Celtic Carved Lovespoons: 30 Patterns	Sharon Littley & Clive Griffin
Celtic Woodcraft	Glenda Bennett
Complete Woodfinishing (Revised Edition)	Ian Hosker
David Charlesworth's Furniture–Making Techniques	
	David Charlesworth
David Charlesworth's Furniture–Making Techniques – Volume 2	
	David Charlesworth
Furniture–Making Projects for the Wood Craftsman	
	GMC Publications
Furniture–Making Techniques for the Wood Craftsman	
	GMC Publications
Furniture Projects with the Router	Kevin Ley
Furniture Restoration (Practical Crafts)	Kevin Jan Bonner
Furniture Restoration: A Professional at Work	John Lloyd
Furniture Restoration and Repair for Beginners	Kevin Jan Bonner
Furniture Restoration Workshop	Kevin Jan Bonner
Green Woodwork	Mike Abbott
Intarsia: 30 Patterns for the Scrollsaw	John Everett
Kevin Ley's Furniture Projects	Kevin Ley
Making Chairs and Tables – Volume 2	GMC Publications
Making Classic English Furniture	Paul Richardson
Making Heirloom Boxes	Peter Lloyd
Making Screw Threads in Wood	Fred Holder
Making Woodwork Aids and Devices	Robert Wearing
Mastering the Router	Ron Fox
Pine Furniture Projects for the Home	Dave Mackenzie
Router Magic: Jigs, Fixtures and Tricks to	
Unleash your Router's Full Potential	Bill Hylton
Router Projects for the Home	GMC Publications
Router Tips & Techniques	Robert Wearing
Routing: A Workshop Handbook	Anthony Bailey
Routing for Beginners	Anthony Bailey
Sharpening: The Complete Guide	Jim Kingshott
Space–Saving Furniture Projects	Dave Mackenzie
Stickmaking: A Complete Course	Andrew Jones & Clive George
Stickmaking Handbook	Andrew Jones & Clive George
Storage Projects for the Router	GMC Publications
Veneering: A Complete Course	Ian Hosker
Veneering Handbook	Ian Hosker
Woodworking Techniques and Projects	Anthony Bailey
Woodworking with the Router: Professional	
Router Techniques any Woodworker can Use	
	Bill Hylton & Fred Matlack

VIDEOS

Drop–in and Pinstuffed Seats	David James	Twists and Advanced Turning	Dennis White
Stuffover Upholstery	David James	Sharpening the Professional Way	Jim Kingshott
Elliptical Turning	David Springett	Sharpening Turning & Carving Tools	Jim Kingshott
Woodturning Wizardry	David Springett	Bowl Turning	John Jordan
Turning Between Centres: The Basics	Dennis White	Hollow Turning	John Jordan
Turning Bowls	Dennis White	Woodturning: A Foundation Course	Keith Rowley
Boxes, Goblets and Screw Threads	Dennis White	Carving a Figure: The Female Form	Ray Gonzalez
Novelties and Projects	Dennis White	The Router: A Beginner's Guide	Alan Goodsell
Classic Profiles	Dennis White	The Scroll Saw: A Beginner's Guide	John Burke

MAGAZINES

WOODTURNING ◆ WOODCARVING ◆ FURNITURE & CABINETMAKING ◆ THE ROUTER ◆ NEW WOODWORKING
THE DOLLS' HOUSE MAGAZINE ◆ OUTDOOR PHOTOGRAPHY ◆ BLACK & WHITE PHOTOGRAPHY ◆ KNITTING
TRAVEL PHOTOGRAPHY ◆ MACHINE KNITTING NEWS ◆ GUILD OF MASTER CRAFTSMEN NEWS

The above represents a selection of titles currently published or scheduled to be published.
All are available direct from the Publishers or through bookshops, newsagents and specialist retailers.
To place an order, or to obtain a complete catalogue, contact:
GMC Publications,
Castle Place, 166 High Street, Lewes, East Sussex BN7 1XU United Kingdom
Tel: 01273 488005 Fax: 01273 402866 E–mail: pubs@thegmcgroup.com
Orders by credit card are accepted